EVERY DAY IS
A HIGH HOLY DAY

Stories of an Adventuring Spirit

Ernie Hawks

ISBN-13: 978-0692027974
MichalHawks Publishing
All photos © by Ernie Hawks
unless otherwise noted
Cover photo © by John Brierley,
Back cover photo of Alice Lindy Lake
and Lester Pass by Ernie Hawks
inset photo © by Britton Bostick
All photos used with permission

Perry
we are one
thank you
Ernie Hawks

DEDICATION
TO MY LOVELY AND SUPPORTIVE WIFE LINDA MICHAL
WHO STOOD BY ME AND ENCOURAGED ME THROUGH
THIS PROJECT NEVER LETTING ME WAVER. THANK YOU
LINDA.

Every Day is a High Holy Day

Table of Contents

ACKNOWLEDGMENTS

Many thanks to my dear friend Trish Gannon publisher of *The River Journal*. Her encouragement, the reminders of deadlines, the teasing, prodding, and skillful editing kept me on track.

Marilyn Rousher for her reading and valued comments.

John Brierly, who took a beautiful photo for the cover of this book of me near the Titcomb Basin. Thanks John for the proof I really was there.

Of course I want to recognize Noah and Ana Huston for allowing me to write so many stories about their family, I love you all.

And there are all of you who have been my hiking companions over the years. Some I have mentioned on these pages. Your help in my "research" has been a joy even while we ate, yet another, dehydrated meal or dry energy bar as we made our way on the trail.

I must mention my Spiritual mentors but the list would be long. Thomas Merton said "every moment and every event of every man's life on earth plants something in his soul." How true.

So if I do a list I'm sure I would miss several and not know where to stop. Of those I could name, there are some who have used all of their teaching skills hoping against hope I would finally get it. In fact, they sometimes needed a "Cosmic 2X4" to get my attention. Others would be surprised and amused that I would consider them for a list of Spiritual coaches, and more who would be offended to be on such a list.

But I thank each and every one. You all have changed my life.

Foreword

Everyone has stories and each story has meaning to others. These are some of my stories and I hope you find meaning in reading them. I also hope it will encourage you to share your stories because they are valuable.

Meaning Making connects us to each other, builds relationships and helps us understand our oneness.

Thanks and enjoy.
Ernie
Athol, Idaho 2014

I know it sounds odd, but it looked as if she was posing.

A Divine Appointment

I had spent the night camped on the Vermilion River in Canada's Kootenay National Park and was headed for Jasper National Park. My search to find, and photograph, caribou was about to begin.

The season was mid fall, and this was a solo trip into the Canadian Rockies looking for these big and rather rare animals.

As with every trip of this nature, personal and spiritual growth was part of my intention.

I knew I was in both grizzly and black bear country and honestly hoped to avoid them. Several times last summer my wife

Linda and I knew bears had visited our home in the Idaho woods. They had destroyed and emptied bird feeders, left signs and prints in the yard. There had also been one close, but still safe, sighting while on an extended back pack trip with friends. Those experiences affirmed my reason to be cautious, as well as conscious that we share the same habitat.

In some native cultures Bear represents introspection, sometimes called the Dreamtime. With Bear we can feel a kinship; it is an omnivore as we are, and it can stand and function on two legs as we do. With Bear we also think of hibernation - going within. With each bear encounter I am reminded of the importance of doing just that, of listening to the voice of Spirit within.

Driving up along the river toward Vermilion Pass and the Continental Divide, I kept seeing places my attention was drawn to, but tried to ignore the invitations in my rush to get farther north.

The Canadian Rockies are filled with beautiful and unique geological formations. The park rangers have made a point of making sure each traveler is aware of them all. However, my single focus of the day was to get to Caribou country so I did my best to pay no heed to them.

Due to my morning cup of coffee and not far into the trip, I was forced to stop at Numa Falls to use the privy. As I was walking back to the car, the liquid voice of the nearby hydraulics was an invitation to take the short hike to its source. In these mountains, waterfalls appear way too frequently to stop for all of them, but this time I surrendered to the suggestion.

I am glad I listened. A footbridge crossed the narrow chasm where the stream dropped several feet. Standing on it I felt the power of water as it sanded out round, smooth bowls in the rocks on both sides of the noisy cascade. It was a good place to take a respite from driving and to feel the soft refreshing spray on my face. I was invigorated and refreshed by the strength and gentleness of water.

Back at the car, the biggest raven I have ever seen landed

on the ground beside me. I know these mysterious black birds are used to people and expect to get handouts, but this guy was big. I grabbed a camera, snapped off a couple shots, and got ready to drive.

The unfed raven hopped onto the hood and tried to convince me he needed payment for the pictures. I found it amusing but started the motor anyway. The noise spooked the big bird and he flew. I thought about raven medicine and wondered why it had been presented to me in such an "in my face" way.

Raven represents heightened awareness and greater understanding of our consciousness, and is sometimes called magic, sometimes called Spirit. Raven asks us to experience the transformation it brings to our multidimensional self. It also reminds us to reunite with the mysteries of the universe so we can expel our inner demons.

Even though the short side trip was fascinating, I felt I had wasted some time. However, while driving I heard Raven say, "The intended use of this trip is a personal and spiritual journey, so listen to that inner voice. It is about the journey." Hmm, is that some sort of life lesson? Is my rush to reach a destination rather than be in the journey an inner demon?

Christina Baldwin says in *Life's Companion*, "I do not possess either past or the future, where I seem to spend so much of my time. In other words, I have been nowhere, because there is nowhere but here/now."

In a few miles, a sign beckoned to another roadside attraction, this time Marble Canyon. Now, in these rugged hills, beautiful dramatic canyons are as common as waterfalls, oftentimes coupled together. But some mystery – possibly Raven – made the call strong, so I stopped.

Marble Canyon is a short deep slot created by Tokumm Creek flowing through an ancient terminal moraine.

It appears to be a deep crevice, but is actually a gorge carved by years of aqua-colored, glacial water etching limestone and white dolomite, giving it the look of marble – thus the name.

As I looked into the ravine, studying the secrets in the spray- shrouded slot, I saw boulders that had fallen and been wedged into the narrow crack sometimes a hundred feet from the bottom. Vegetation, fed by the fog of the torrents below, now grows on them.

Natural bridges straddle the abyss, where the water had first flowed over rock, until the rasping of the glacial till in the surging icy melt excavated a channel under the lip, blasting out a hole and leaving an arch.

Water is cleansing, powerful and subtle, sometimes called the universal solvent. It can change a landscape in seconds or spend thousands of years slowly, persistently changing a scene. It also feeds and nurtures the growth of plants and animals. It is a necessity for life that can also destroy it - a study in polarities.

For me, it is easier to be present when I'm in nature. My senses are drawn to the energy of the natural world. It is so much bigger than me or even my imagination, yet I know I am part of it. I often use these lessons to keep a perspective. I am reminded no matter how it is being used – each moment is a precious moment.

After hiking up and back on a trail that criss-crossed the ravine on foot bridges for a little over an hour, I was back at the car. It felt good to have fresh air in my lungs and the enjoyment of another exceptional geological feature. And, I still felt the need to be going.

There was very light traffic on the road while climbing beside the river toward the pass. I kept thinking about getting to Jasper and the caribou, wondering why I had been so easily distracted. However, it was still early and the light was good if another photo op was presented.

Alone on the road and nearing the top, I saw something walking, crossing the yellow center line, maybe a half mile ahead. I slowed a little but kept going, my curiosity becoming piqued.

I rolled on, watching, wondering, until I was close enough

to identify the Grizzly bear angling across the road looking directly at me. The sun was backlighting its long guard hairs giving it that grizzled look and its name. Not huge but full-grown, I think it was a female.

I stopped. She was looking through the windshield - into me - and continued for several more steps. Then she turned slightly and headed off the road to my right, allowing me to see that distinct Grizzly profile, the shoulder hump, the dished line between the eyes and nose. She continued to maintain eye contact with me until she all but disappeared in the woody brush.

I powered down the right side window hoping for a picture without getting out. The foliage did not allow a shot so I cautiously got out on the left side, camera in hand, and leaned on the hood where the raven had earlier scolded me.

She stopped and turned, looked at me a moment, then wandered toward the river. The brush nearly concealed her and I could only see movement through the branches. She stood tall enough to look at me again, I think to see if I was still watching. Still it wasn't a clear shot, even when I manually focused on her through the nearly bare brushwood between us. I was thoroughly enjoying the encounter, and was still alone with her.

After her look she disappeared; I wondered if she was fishing or sitting in the water. A car stopped and the passenger asked what was up. I said I thought there was a Grizzly in the river. They asked if I could see it and I said not very well. They looked and then moved on. I was alone with her again – good.

In a short time - it seemed forever - she crawled up the steep bank on the opposite side. Sure enough she had been sitting in the stream, wet from the waist down. With her hair smoothed by the water she looked like she was wearing a pair of dripping wet pants.

The climb brought her back up to my elevation. As soon as I had a clear shot, I reset the auto focus and started snapping away. Fortunately, the telephoto lens I happened to have on at the time was perfect for the distance.

She stopped and looked back. I know it sounds odd, but it looked as if she was posing, stopping, moving slowly, stepping onto a log and waiting. I popped open the shutter dozens of times, taking advantage of each position. I felt there had been a prearranged appointment for this encounter. Maybe that explained all the mysterious distractions of the morning - a divine appointment.

Ms. Griz, across the way, seemed to sense it was time to go and headed up the hill into some scrub.

I took a deep breath.

The bear moved in and out of sight for a while and was gone. The last time I saw her she stopped and looked back; again I felt she was looking into me. I thanked her for the time and the pictures she had allowed.

Back in the car, introspection was in the front of my mind. It had been a morning of listening to my inner voice and being in the moment with each click of the shutter. The reward: an early morning misty face wash, an entertaining and enlightening visit with a raven, a refreshing walk on the lip of a deep narrow gorge, and some communion time alone with a grizzly.

I spent the next week hiking, waiting, searching, but there was not a trace of caribou, and no one else had seen any. Yet by being present, each precious moment was a Divine Appointment.

Those huge granite towers are scarred and scored by the ice fields.

Collective Creativity

The fast flowing stream cascaded through a narrow chute; everything was frozen but the falls. Fog created by mist was rising from the torrent. I sat absorbed by the Spirit of the mountains when Elk came into view across the creek. Vapor wafted from his nostrils as he moved along the brook. His breath and mine mixed with the spray between us over the water, becoming one. I could see how we are related, connected by the one thing our life depends on more than any other – our breath, Holy air, the Great Spirit.

Spirit breathes us while Breath creates life all around us. More than anything else it unites us with all of creation. We share it with everything: the plants, the animals, even the earth itself. The very essence of the air is more than the sum of its parts; a mystery no living being can survive without for more than a few minutes.

Realizing that breathing is a sacred practice may be one of my most powerful inspirations. In many faith traditions, spirit also means breath or wind. Our word spirit is derived from the Latin *spiritus*, which means breath. *Pneuma* is Greek for the spirit, a term which also means breath. The Hebrew word *Ruah* is synonymous with wind.

But this concept is not unique to these languages. There are words, or their derivations, in the Buddhist teaching, the Upanishads and other Sanskrit writings that mean the same as spirit, breath or wind.

Which begs the question for me, can this constant be by chance? Or is it the Christ energy making it clear, through the collective creativity of several languages - to know the breath is to know Spirit?

As these questions weigh on my mind I breathe, and re-breathe, re-breathe Spirit, re-Spirit, respirate - respiration is the act of breathing Spirit as Spirit breathes me.

I was taught God was a man like Superman sitting on a throne far away in a palace called Heaven. Now I understand God as energy, bigger than I can imagine, yet I am part of it.

Science is proving there is connectivity between all things at the molecular level. People who said there is no God are now proving this energy which is as old as the Big Bang and as present as today. It is that big; and it is as simple as our breath.

While backpacking with friends in the Wind River Range in Wyoming a new perspective of breathing became present. We had hiked for a week mostly between 10,500 feet and 11,500 feet.

That isn't high as far as world elevations go, but it is higher than I am used to. It turned into a week of conscious breathing.

To prepare for the hike, we camped between 7,000 and 8,000 feet for a few days, with day hikes well into the tens.

The last couple of nights before we started were spent at the trailhead near 9,500 feet. With that training, we managed to convince ourselves our lungs were ready for the thinner air, and confidently headed out on a seven day trek.

In four miles of pleasant, forested walking we had gained over 1,000 feet and rest was necessary. We stopped at a spot called (with very good reason) Photographer's Point.

We were feeling the strain but doing fine in the thin air until the vistas took our breath away.

Several gray, stony spires pierced the sky still gripping, against the forces of time, snippets of ancient glaciers. We could see into valley bottoms less than 7,000 feet and up to peaks over 13,500.

While standing and looking I noticed my breathing. Usually, I take it for granted, but at this altitude it was ever present.

There would be several breaks during the next week, both to draw in the precious views of nature and to draw in the precious gift of nature, breath.

After a half hour at Photographer's Point we continued walking and with each breath there was a message from my lungs: "We could use a little more."

Deep into valleys with stream crossings it was there. Up over saddles and through gaps it was there. To the tree line and beyond it was there. Always I was feeling my lungs asking for just a little more.

One morning there was frost on our tents and the vegetation around us. The water supply drawn from the lake the night before was frozen. Crawling out into the new day I could see my breath. It joined my companions' breath and then united with the atmosphere around us.

It reminded me of the American Indians and their use of the peace pipe. As they pass the pipe they exhale the smoke. The smoke symbolizes the individual's Spirit mingling with others and dissipating into the all.

We are taught to breathe whenever life's tensions materialize. It is the very act of consciously breathing that centers us with Spirit – the breath of Spirit. With it we are connected to the ancient, the present and the future.

We spent several days at the higher elevations of the Wind River Range never quite acclimating to the thinner air. So the awareness of our breathing was always there. Still the beauty of the place, the pristine lakes, pure tumbling streams, and those huge granite towers scarred and scored by the ice fields of centuries ago kept taking our breath away.

It was a week-long reminder, through Spirit, that as we breathe we are connected to other humans, other animals, the Earth and all she supports. We are individual creations that make up one vast creation.

To be in the mountain wilderness, in its silence and in its darkness, gave me pause enough to explore my humanness and my spiritualness, where the Universal Love screams through the silence and shines through the darkness.

While writing it is not unusual to feel words are coming through me – almost like I am breathing them. It is a good and loving feeling recognizing the awareness of my connection to Spirit. Regardless of whether it is called Universal Intelligence, Collective Creativity, or The Force, it doesn't matter. When I am aware of that presence it feels as if It is breathing me. It is difficult finding words to describe what It is. That image of a Superman in the heavens definitely is not what It is.

Like the breezes blowing through the crowns of the trees, this energy is only heard. However, it is constantly speaking to creation and, with words and thoughts, to people and through people.

These words, these thoughts, these inspirations, are given to all of us. How many times has there been an insight, an a-ha? A-ha is not really a word but a breath – Spirit breathing.

Inspiration, slightly misspelled, can be in-spirit-ation - an A-ha. Is that coincidence?

Astronomer Harlow Shapley has calculated that some of the atoms we breathe today we will re-breathe one year from now no matter where we are on Earth. He also pointed out we are constantly breathing the same atoms Gandhi, Buddha, and Jesus breathed in their lifetimes.

These atoms have experienced evolution from pre-history to the present. There is an ever expanding intelligence in the universe moving us to a higher state of intellect or enlightenment.

When the seed was set by John F. Kennedy to send a man to the moon many thought to be impossible. But with that concept came a focus and discovery until we set foot on the moon.

No doubt mistakes were made, discoveries that did not work. Each of them was a reward, as they let us know one more system that did not work. Knowing how to do something right requires knowing what is wrong.

This evolution of concept to discovery and focus until we reach the goal is Collective Creativity, or Universal Intelligence,

That explains why there is something bigger than even a Superman sitting in a palace far away. This explains a Universal Creativity I am part of. This explains the bigness I am connected to through my inner self, my Spiritual self. and to awaken to this bigness is as ancient, as rudimentary, as common, and as necessary as breathing.

Going to the top of a mountain or sharing a misty breath with an elk by a stream is not required. All that is necessary is to breathe, to center in that breath, to re-Spirit, to respirate, to receive in-spirit-ation, the a-ha.

13

Every day, every minute, we breathe Holy Air. It is necessary for this human life, it is necessary for our Spiritual life, and it is our connection to our Collective Creativity.

We are all warmed by the same sun
We all rest under the same moon
We all breathe the same air
I will not let the soil you stand on define me.

Beyond were numerous peaks reaching heights of over 13,500 feet creating the Continental Divide and a cirque that held Titcomb Basin.

A Humbling Reward

From a notch above Little Seneca Lake on the Highline trail I scanned across Island Lake to the glacial-polished, granite ridge on the other side. Beyond were numerous peaks reaching heights of over 13,500 feet creating the Continental Divide and a cirque that held Titcomb Basin—our goal for the day.

It was our third day in the Wind River Range. The Basin had drawn us to west central Wyoming and "The Winds," as the locals call them.

Now, after weeks of planning and several days of acclimating to the altitude, we could only see an outline of the towers. Smoke from wildfires to the west screened the details and filtered the view of the sculpted cliffs.

There was some grousing among us about the haze. However, we also had heard of the storms that blow in the Winds, which can make a trek like ours above the tree line look as flat as Kansas. At least we could see mountains in the cloud and we were appreciative.

From this vantage point in the gap we still could not see into the carved bowl. It would be another four miles around Island Lake and over a couple of moraines to reach that famous destination. However, this overlook could have been an excellent destination in itself.

There had been other panoramas along the way and every time I was struck by our differing reactions to the same sights.

Each of us has seen dramatic landscapes. John has scaled the mountains of Switzerland, New Zealand and others around the world. Andrew has climbed in the Himalayas, Alaska, and Mexico as well the U.S. and Canada. I have hiked above and below the glaciers of the Canadian Rockies and the ranges in the Northwest United States. The three of us have history, yet every time we arrive at a new vista we are first-timers.

I know part of our disappointment with the pollution from the fires was the desire to see the subtleties of the cliffs and gorges. The challenge of a good backpack trip is always part of a journey like this, yet it is the sights that motivate the expedition.

The poor visibility did not keep us from following the rocky trail into the canyon, skirting the lake and climbing up around the crests. Still, we hoped the winds this range is famous for would come and blow the smoke away.

The trail is well defined but difficult to negotiate due to rocks—it is impossible to set a rhythm. So with a cadence of trip, slip, sidestep, high step, ankle roll we made slow progress.

Around us was scarred granite with barely enough soil for short vegetation. We marveled at the fact that anything could grow at all, but green was almost as prominent as the speckled granular stone on the landscape. On both sides of the trail scratches from ancient ice flows marred the otherwise smooth roundness of the valley floors. The track traversed a slope onto a moraine. There, at

10,800 feet we got our first glimpse into Titcomb Basin and its lakes. Titcomb Lakes are a series of small, shallow tarns. Some flow from one to the other over very gentle cascades, nearly as wide as the ponds they separate. They drop, only a couple feet, into a lower clear, azure-blue mere. Narrow streams flow into small ravines, through gracefully rounded base rocks that connect them to other pools in the chain.

Erratics, some as big as trucks, left from the melting glaciers, were scattered about like toys on the floor of a child's play room waiting to be put away.

We became quiet as we tried to comprehend the magnitude of the cirque and all it held.

John's wonder at the harsh beauty reminded me of my granddaughter as she discovers each new flower or blade of grass in our woods. Dropping his pack, and with camera in hand, he shot from every perspective all the while savoring, marveling at it all. It looked to me like he wanted to keep it or, at least, reach out and touch it.

Andrew, more analytical, studied every crag, each hanging valley, all of the cols between the crests of the stark rock faces soaring over three thousand feet above us. Map in hand he compared the topography to the paper in his lap, all while looking for possible routes to make an ascent.

I stood, hopefully unobtrusively, focusing in each direction, looking, raising and lowering my focus, trying to turn something indescribable into words.

I felt I was in The Great Cathedral and didn't want to foul it, by sight or sound, in any way.

The cliffs climbed up from the floor, smooth at first where the glacier had burnished them. Their surfaces became more coarse as they ascended above the former ice flow, the tops left as ragged, irregular pinnacles of stone piercing into bright blue sky.

Each of us in our own way was trying to absorb the entire scene lying before us. Three different approaches and three different experiences of the same place but all with a reverence the Spirit of the Mountains deserves—in fact commands—at a place like this.

Rugged, pristine beauty surrounded us as we gazed in awe. Then, we all noticed, at about the same time, the smoke had lifted. The early morning concerns about not being able to fully experience the scale and scope of the basin had been taken by the winds of The Winds. It felt as if a divine gift had been given to us unnoticed while we had been marching, with attention to passage, into this glorious place.

That is when we all reacted the same—with amazing thankfulness at this extraordinary and humbling reward.

Each time that moose drool flowed back into the pond. I thought about
the beer by that name and could not stop a smile.

Patience and Presents

The big cow moose looked up from the water where she
was drinking—or eating, I could not tell which—directly at me.
Since it was rutting season in the mountains where I hiked, I
checked to make sure there wasn't a bull I hadn't detected. I'm
never comfortable between two lovers and when they are moose
I'm less comfortable. He wasn't present, for now, and she studied
me carefully before retuning her snout to the water. When she
looked up again gallons of fresh moose drool appeared.

The day had started, for me, just before the sky over the Canadian Rockies became light. As I shed the sleeping bag, October frosty air raised goose bumps on my bare legs. The night before I made sure long johns were only a quick grab away. In a few seconds, I was in them, and then fully dressed in a few more.

After firing the Jetboil stove to heat coffee water, I had to go out and deal with another early morning detail.

The SUV is a good little camper, for one person, and, on this morning, I took full advantage of one important feature —the heater. By the time the engine was running and the heater turned on, the coffee water was hot. I was ready for a good day to begin.

I was "road hunting" with my camera and being self-contained in the car made breaking camp easy. A little granola, a travel cup full of java, and I began adventuring.

The day before I experienced a "Rocky Mountain High" that still had me floating; I spent time with, and photographed, a Grizzly. Last night I downloaded the images onto my computer, which launched the delight all over again. I was excited for what this day would bring.

Driving into the Maligne Valley my hope was to see some caribou, which sometimes hang out there, but the success of the trip was not dependent on a sighting—the Spirit of the mountains took care of that.

That Spirit is easy to know in the Maligne. High, saw-tooth-shaped peaks, some with natural arches, cast early morning shadows across the canyon. Their glacial-scraped, raw faces created an imposing east wall above the tree line.

A coyote, The Trickster, trotted along the side of the road. I pulled up a camera for a shot out the window but he turned and only showed me his bushy tail. That has been my experience with them. I had been tricked again.

From a hill above Medicine Lake, I could see a bull moose flirting with a cow in the water. The morning light and the distance only allowed dark silhouettes of their cavorting.

Moose are rather ungainly looking. Their legs are too skinny and there is that odd shaped body with a huge head and rack that looks to tip them over. They look like they are made out of spare parts. Yet, Miss Lady Cow moose seemed attracted. He assumed a regal pose, head high, walking purposely through the water.

Moose Medicine teaches us the value of self-esteem, and of rewarding ourselves and others for a job well done. Moose does not suffer from false shyness or inhibitions or the tendency to make light of his own accomplishments. He is not coy about his successes. Moose says, "I worked hard to do this, and I did it well. I'm proud of myself." Moose knows how damaging unkind criticism and fault-finding is to the spirit of someone trying to learn and do their best.

I accepted that lesson and released my unkind thoughts about the appearance of Moose. I know he did not accept them and I didn't want to own them either.

I stood in the chill for a half hour watching before returning to the heated car. The cold sting of the wind and snow-rain on my face had reminded me of my inner flame. Embracing that flame calls attention to my strength.

By the time I reached Maligne Lake, the sun was warming the valley floor and the spirit of the day had me fully in its grip. I parked at a trailhead and prepared for a short hike to a small lake. A young man vacationing from Berlin was already there. He asked about bears and whether he would be safe. I said making noise is the best thing to do. He headed out while I prepared my daypack.

As I started up the trail, I noticed several tracks of various animals, deer and moose being the most common. Each print had filled with water from rains the day before and frozen during the night. Several minutes later, a little over a mile into the hike, I rounded a bend on the trail in a small, dense cedar grove. There was the fellow I had seen at the trailhead. He was off the track in the trees and hadn't seen me. As I moved closer he seemed a little agitated. When he finally noticed me, his excitement nearly exploded.

"I just saw a moose! I have never seen a moose before, are we safe here?"

I assured him that if it had left we were probably okay for now, but to be very aware. I asked if it was a male or female, and he said, "It didn't have any horns."

I told him I thought there was a pond close and that we may see her again there.

In another mile we were there. I suggested we wait quietly and see if she showed up. He hung around for a couple minutes and said he needed to get back. I said fine, make noise as you go.

I felt a need to stay, so waited in the silence of the forest, all my senses alert. Scanning the area, I saw an active trail into the water on the other side.

Above the forest, I could see one of the saw-tooth peaks reflecting a small ray of morning sun. I snapped the shutter a couple of times and let my focus drop back to the water. A ring from a fish rising appeared. Some small birds, too far away to identify, flitted in brush. My gaze wandered around a bit and back to the trail into the water, and then up, again, to the peak. I looked at some more rings in the water and back to the trail. After about an hour of listening, smelling, feeling and watching I wondered if I had the patience for this either. Once again, I scanned across to the game trail—and there she was.

Her huge moose presence was camouflaged until she wanted me to see her. I felt her Spirit—how she aids in moving emotions to allow for awareness, how she teaches strength, wisdom and patience. There is gentleness in that strength. It's life awakening, and calms any fears I had. Still, with the rut on in the mountains, I knew part of the lesson, her wisdom, was to be very conscious while not allowing trepidation to control me.

She waded in my direction, dipping her snout and looking up. Each time moose drool flowed back into the pond. I thought about the beer by that name and could not stop a smile.

Time went fast and she gave me several good poses, moving close before heading up the hill on the trail I had followed to the pond. She looked back once before her camouflage took her quietly and quickly out of sight and sound.

The trail looped back to where I parked in another direction, and knowing she might be going to meet a male, I took that route. Later in the day, while passing a small store, I thought a beer sounded good, rather unusual for a cool day.

She looked back once before her camouflage took her quietly and quickly out of sight and sound.

We put it in the corner where the side without branches could not be seen.

Angel on Top of the Tree
The First Christmas in a Relationship

This Christmas is proving to be a little different. The changes started last spring, when Linda found a cute cabin on a small mountain lake and decided it was about the most perfect place to live - I came with the cabin.

Of course, since I had spent a few years in this place and in these woods, I also think it is the most perfect place to live, and now, to share with her.

So how will Christmas be different? Well, I'm not sure yet, but I've seen some signs it may be. One is the way the house is being decorated. I always decorated by writing "Merry XMAS" in the dust on top of some unused surface, if I could find one. Then when I did my spring cleaning I put away the decorations. Sometimes, of course, spring cleaning came in August, when someone was coming to visit. Now, cut boughs are being hung on the walls where things used to grow naturally.

Cutting a Christmas tree always seemed rather redundant. I always had several different kinds of vegetation in various stages of dying sitting around gasping for air and water. But this year, there is a tree.

However we didn't use the tree we had originally planned on. Last fall we found a perfect one up in the hills behind the cabin. It was in a group of other trees about the same size. Knowing that many would not survive, we planned on cutting one for Christmas.

One morning in mid December, after some new powder fell, it was time to head out to get the tree. We strapped on the snowshoes and took the old plastic Torpedo sled that looks like a big blue plate along with us. It is used around the place to bring in wood and haul out garbage. Now, it would haul the tree.

Being the youthful fifty-somethings that we are, when we came to a perfect sledding hill, we had to try it. In just two runs, Linda got the award for going the fastest—her hair was straight back. I got the award for going the farthest, because of extra weight that came with my new diet, which has improved since last spring. Linda also got the award for doing the most damage to a tree, which became the one we weren't planning on using.

I made a run, and then it was Linda's turn. She took off her snowshoes and put them under her on the sled for the walk back up the hill. When she asked how to steer, I said, "It will kind of go where you want. Just follow my trail." She then started down the same track I had made, now packed for faster sledding. A short way down, she left the sloping ridge my path was on and took a short cut down the side. This course was steeper and had a few moguls. On the first mogul, gravity lost a battle with the sled, the snowshoes and Linda. As she was flying over the terrain, I was quite impressed by her speed. I immediately conceded the contest to her.

Her speed was impressive as were her shrieks; however, I think if she had closed her mouth as well as those big, dark brown eyes, and tucked in her hair, she might have gained a bit more momentum.

About halfway down the slope a Douglas fir was awakened from its winter dormancy by an airborne sled with a middle-aged lady passenger flying over it, and two snowshoes following close behind her. The snowshoes, from the tree's perspective, looked like weird, distorted wings, making the whole scene look rather like a freakish angel on a plate, swooping down at cosmic speed, sounding similar to a siren during a power surge. The tree took a direct hit and lay down half buried in the previous night's flurries. As the angel went over, one of the loose snowshoes stuck in the snow, looking like a strange tombstone.

Linda stopped shortly after she started up the other side of the ravine. When I got to her, she was still sitting on the buried sled with her legs hidden under the snow. At first I thought she had lost her eyelids, but then they slowly reemerged from deep within her sockets. She did suffer from some hyper-extended vocal chords and a little windburn on her face, but nothing else.

When we climbed back up to the tree now completely removed from its roots, Linda insisted we couldn't cut a second tree as this one was already down. I was glad she hadn't hit the young tamarack a few feet away.

We didn't put the tree in front of the bay window where it could be admired from all sides, as planned. We put it in the corner where the side without branches, some of which might still be flying from the impact with the sled, could not be seen.

On Christmas day we will enjoy our tree, the decorations and a big meal with family and friends, while listening to music of the season from the stereo sitting on a shiny clean surface. We will be celebrating the new beginnings that this time of year is about.

And, in Christmases to come, the angel at the top of the tree will forever hold a new meaning.

The textures of those greens included everything from lacy boughs to long needles.

Climbing to Clear Skies

The day dawned with bright sunshine on the bay in front of Ana and Noah's apartment. Across the water was Port Orchard and behind it, in the distance, Mt. Rainer was wearing her pink robe of morning sun.

As Noah fixed coffee it was easy to see his excitement. "It's going to be a great day up on Hurricane Ridge," he grinned.

Linda and I had driven over to see their first apartment the week after Christmas, a time of year when no one can count on a sunny day.

The only disappointing part of the day was that Ana, Linda's daughter, had to work and couldn't go with us. So after she caught the ferry to Seattle, we started the two-hour drive to Port Angeles, then up to our destination.

The Olympic Peninsula was saturated with green. Puget Sound rains had left all the trees damp, making the colors vibrant

29

and almost shiny as we drove north past the Bangor Submarine Base.

Noah's enthusiasm to show us someplace we had never seen was fun to watch. Linda and I had driven around the Olympic Range and we had looked up at the snow-covered crowns from the ferry in the middle of the Sound, but had never been into the mountains. Hurricane Ridge is one of the few places you can drive to at the very edge of the wilderness.

As we drove, clouds started to appear in the brilliant blue sky. We passed Sequim and commented about how it is often mispronounced. (If you have never been there, it has only one syllable.)

There was still a feeling of exhilaration in the car. Linda and I were going to a place we had always wanted to see and Noah was getting to show off one of his favorite playgrounds.

For a while the sky was blue with some gray, but as we wound around the peninsula it started to become gray with some blue. Noah watched the sky and I thought I saw a bit of disappointment in him as I took off my now unneeded, sunglasses. I wanted to let him know that we could still have a good time with a low soggy ceiling. I spotted a local winery and said we would need to stop on our way back. That got a smile out of him.

By the time we were in Port Angeles the sky had fallen. The town was so socked in it was hard to see the end of the piers along the waterfront.

At one of the main intersections we took a left and were on the road to Hurricane Ridge. I was still quite excited about finally getting to see it, but as we started to climb the fog got thicker until we could hardly see the tops of the grand old trees along the way.

Noah was now voicing his disappointment in the day.

As I looked at the murkiness swirling around us, I remembered a similar drive Linda and I had taken a few years ago. It was my chance to show her the Ross Creek Cedars above Bull Lake in Montana. She had never been there. As we drove along the valley floor the clouds settled down upon us. I was looking forward to showing her the view of the mountains across the valley as we ascended out of the canyon toward the grove. But on that day we couldn't see across the road, let alone across the valley. Just as we reached the last possible vista we would get, we came out above the fog. The mountains jutted out of the heavy vapor we had driven through and glistened in the bright sun shining out of a blue Montana sky. I wondered if the same might happen in the Olympic Range.

Noah was trying to be upbeat, but I sensed he was feeling the thickness of the weather we were in. Then, almost like driving through a wall, the atmosphere we had been in cleared. The only thing between us and miles of panorama was clear mountain air.

We pulled off the road at the first chance to see what we had climbed through. All around us were hills and ridges. Below us the heavy fog we had been in was a beautiful, white angora blanket. The blanket had tucked itself into all the valleys leaving a skirt that fluffed out across the Strait of Juan de Fuca. We couldn't see Victoria, BC to the north, hidden under the gauzy white, but on the horizon to the east was Mt. Baker in the Cascade Range.

The spruces, pines, hemlocks, cedars, firs and more each gave us their interpretation of green. The textures, everything from lacy boughs, to long needles, gave every slope its own character. The vivid blue above was a contrast to the rain forest that surrounded us, and the soft white below.

The brightest thing I saw was Noah's face. His passion for the day was back. I was as glad for him that the fog had stayed below, as I was to see this new place. I put my sunglasses back on.

We drove on up the road. Winter in the Pacific Northwest was considerably warmer than usual that late December day. And, as one would expect, there was much less snow than normal. This became obvious as we passed snow removal equipment parked along the road, waiting to be used. The apparatus was really just a self-propelled snow blower, one that could chew through a ten foot snow drift and blow it hundreds of feet off the road into the gorge below. But, setting there in about four inches of snow, it looked like a severe case of overkill, somewhat like showing up at a whistle-whittling contest with a broadsword and battle-axe.

The road ended at the edge of the wilderness area. It was a 17 mile drive up and 5,500 feet of elevation from Port Angeles. Looking around we saw ridge stacked upon ridge with glacier-bearing peaks scattered around just for accent.

We spent some time strolling through the woods, up and over one thrilling view, and then another. We weren't there long, maybe a couple of hours, just long enough for us to want to go back. Go back either with snowshoes, or hiking boots and packs, depending on the time of year. Noah shared his stories of hiking over the crests between the valleys and I could easily understand his love for the place.

Going down the road, we enjoyed the scenery from the opposite angle until we entered the thick murkiness. The sunglasses were once again stored over the visor.

We did stop at that winery and tasted some of their reds. My favorite was a Nouveau Syrah. We bought a couple of bottles and headed back to Ana and Noah's charming first apartment over the bay.

We had just had an introduction to someplace we knew we would get to know much better.

The winery is on the outskirts of Sequim or Squim as the locals call it.

It is one of our favorite short hikes.

Intention and an Adventuring Spirit

Years ago, I heard there was a path up the mountain south of Round Lake, sometimes called "heart attack hike." Finally, my wife, Linda, and I were going to get to the top of it.

Starting the day meant taking the well-maintained trail out of the state park of the same name and around the lake. It is one of our favorite short walks through cedar groves and wetlands, along the lakeshore and past beaver activity. It gives us a good dose of

33

nature without much effort. It was the day to leave that trail and take a chance on that heart attack—Linda and I were not very worried.

The track follows an old abandoned road for a while and we understood it would pass a trailhead that would let us challenge our coronary strength. We could not find any sign of a trail; still our intention was to have a fun day hiking someplace we had never explored.

We wandered through a valley along a small stream with occasional ponds surrounded by skunk cabbage and ferns. Wetlands surrounded by cottonwood and birch flanked our way.

As we walked, we talked about a change coming in our life. Linda's daughter and son-in-law were expecting the following December. We had noticed our attention had shifted a bit. We seemed to notice baby stuff a lot. I found myself checking out some cool rocking animals created by a local woodworker. Normally, I am only looking at his furniture and wood sculptures. Linda bought some onesies at a yard sale—I didn't know what they were. Our conversations were centered more and more on things that needed to be finished around the house. The need to baby-proof became a common topic around the dinner table. And I found myself wondering what it would be like to be a grandfather.

After following the road for nearly an hour, we were wondering about the trail. The sounds of the highway and the railroad were penetrating into the sounds of the forest where we walked, but there was no sign or any indication of a heart stopping trail.

Finally, Linda said, "This looks like a good place to start up." Even though it looked just like the last mile or so. She was right. We had intended to hike to the top of the mountain and why should we not, just because we couldn't find the path.

Our lungs required us to focus on the task at hand; heading straight up the hill, picking our way over blow downs and through brush, making an ascent that was not marked. The search for a trail had changed, but our intention was still focused on summiting.

Stopping for a bite to eat on a small bench, Linda sat on a rock in the shade, and our dog Nikki, who accompanied us on most trips, laid beside her. I wandered around looking for a way off the bench that would take us closer the top. We didn't want to go back the way we came. We had climbed up a steep, rock-covered east face to get to where we were only to find the same down on the west. After some exploring, I found a small saddle, which would take us to the main mountain.

There is quite a sense of personal satisfaction when, even though there have been some roadblocks in the way, you can find a way to accomplish your intention. I don't remember who said it, but there is a quote stating scientists can only be successful through their failures. How many of us have been taught that it is okay to fail? With that attitude I must have learned a lot over the years.

From the top we took a different route down the hill. Part way down we took a break under a big grandfather tree. To me, they represent old, loving energy; energy that provides support for younger growth with its shade and the way it blocks the wind and weather.

I have learned of cultures who bestow the title Grandfather on anyone who shows high spiritual wisdom. It may not be an elder male, but a female, or child could be given the title.

I began to think again about being a grandfather, wondering if I could live up to those traits—either grandfather tree, or Grandfather. Being a grandfather, like the hill we hiked, doesn't seem to have a direct route, a trail, or any directions at all.

However, that may not be a valid concern. Could I be underestimating myself? I had no problem heading up a mountain without a trail, only an intention to have a good day. A day of hiking where we had never been before, a day that may or may not have included reaching the top of the mount.

While sitting under that tree it came to me; it is important for me to take that adventuring spirit into this new era of my life.

The path for me will be an intent to love unconditionally, without knowing what to do or how to do it, which will help me serve this child as a grandfather or as Grandfather.

That is the gift I can give to this child, and the child's gift to me will be this process.

An inglorious end

Lines Creek - Serving a History Lesson

We were just over half way around the three-mile loop, deep in the St. Joe Ranger District, when Linda, a few steps ahead of me on the trail, stopped and said "Oh look." There it was, a steel and iron ghost from the past. Broken and rusty, a derelict left in the woods, the old steam locomotive leaned against a tree.

We had started the day from our camp on Marble Creek just upstream from Donkey Creek. The twelve-mile drive to the trailhead on Forest Service roads had been a breathtaking trip through dense fir and pine stands on steep canyon walls. We drove past expansive views from hundreds of feet above Eagle Creek and across pristine mountain meadows sprinkled with red, yellow, white and purple wild flowers, and small unnamed seasonal streams and ponds. It was midmorning of a rather warm day so, as expected, we didn't see much wildlife, but the sights, sounds and

37

smells were robust.

As we drove we found several camp sites for future trips, even more isolated than where we had spent the last couple of nights. One was next to the road where it crossed Lines Creek. It was also our trailhead.

We were in the "Joe" to see the giant cedars in the Hobo Cedar Grove, but also discovered several historical trails that needed our footprints. One was the Lines Creek Historical trail, considered easy to moderate, and it stimulated our "what's-over-there-itis" which is never quite dormant.

In the early twentieth century, the call of the White pine had brought hundreds of lumberjacks and a few women to the area. At the head of this stream, about a mile and a half from where we started, they had built an incline line.

With trekking poles, some fruit, and water, we headed out. As expected, there were huge White pine stumps with springboard notches three to four feet off the ground. Below the trail were the remains of a flume dam. Where the pond once was, a brushy field grew out of the silt deposits. There were old log chutes and the remains of a fire in 1922.

After about an hour of leisurely hiking and exploring and just before the trail crossed the creek, we saw the remains of the incline line. The "line" was a narrow gauge railroad going straight up the side of the hill. Cars loaded with fresh cut logs were attached to an inch and five-eighths steel cable and pulled by two steam donkeys at the top of the hill. At the top the cars were sent down the other side still attached to the donkey for control.

The incline is not part of the trail we were hiking. Buuut, a serious case of "what's- up- there-itis" got us bad. So, up we went.

Partially buried cable was ever present on, or crossing, the path or, sometimes, wrapped around a tree stump. Big pieces of iron and steel hardware, strewn along the side of the grade, reminded us of the history we were walking through. Rusty barrels leaned against trees while spikes, bolts and bars stuck out of the ground. A recent blow down dropped on the track caused the only turn. Otherwise, it was straight up the hill.

We climbed and rested, then climbed and ate fruit, then climbed and drank water, but regardless of what else we did, we always climbed. The value of switchbacks was an obvious lesson we were experiencing.

Finally, at the top was our reward with views of West Elk Peak and East Elk Peak from the edge of a high jagged rock cliff. We also got a good look at the incline down the other side, but just a look satisfied us this time.

A case of what's-down-there-itis wasn't very severe. Maybe, because we had just climbed over a thousand feet in about three quarters of a mile. As well as knowing that coming back up would be required. So we enjoyed a short rest with some more fruit and water before we started back down the way we came.

As a side note, just below the top we had crossed the road; you know, the kind you drive on. This is not a good time to question our intelligence.

Back at the bottom we crossed Lines Creek and continued on the trail, a little tired but still gripped with "what's-around-the-bend-itis." It was just around the bend where Linda spotted the old locomotive. The only thing left was the cab and boiler, an inglorious end to a once powerful engine that had carried tons of logs, now a relic of scrap iron and boilerplate, being held up by a tree whose parents and grandparents it had hauled away.

Around another few curves were the sixty foot tall remnants of a trestle. These timbers had supported trains 140 to 150 cars long, each car weighing 60 tons or more; now they lean precariously against one another, unable to support anything else.

The trail ended where it began, an easy hike, if you don't do the incline, but with the incline came a deeper understanding of the history.

I may sound impressed, even excited about these relics, and I am. Yet their environmental consequences are not lost on me.

Allowing mountain streambeds to fill with silt due to poorly planned dams, and erosion from putting a trail straight up a steep hill, have left scars that will last longer than the iron and steel rusting away under the trees.

Still, I hope this part of the historic trail will serve a lesson also. These practices were not thought through with future generations in mind.

There was a time when I would get angry over activities from days gone by. Today I know that I can't get angry enough to change anything that was done. So I look with the fascination of an archeologist studying another culture, the fascination of a historian studying the past, and I hope to learn for our grandchildren's sake. Not put my judgment on it, just observe and learn with today's knowledge.

I also hope to learn to check the map for roads before I start up an incline line.

Over it was a log - wet, slippery and appearing to be partially rotted.
(Photo © by Andrew Ashmore)

It is the Journey

There was only a couple miles left but a third of that was across the fast flowing, glacial river Chaba. Once on the other side there was a slight rise over the Continental Divide and then the path down to Fortress Lake—our destination.

Terry started in. Quickly, the swift, glacial-till-filled waters surged over his knees. He stopped, trekking poles in place. He could not see his feet or the river bottom through the milky gray melt. The sand under his feet was washing out, making stability impossible; slowly and carefully he turned back.

Further upstream I was able to walk a bar into the middle of the icy stream but the rest was flowing even faster, and deeper, than Terry's attempt.

Andrew and Jim tried holding arms and going in. With

41

each one using a trekking pole they had six plants in the sandy bottom. With the current lifting up onto their thighs and trying to carry them downstream, due to poor footing, they moved back onto the shallow bar. We all retreated to a higher island in the middle of the riverbed to get our nearly numb feet out of the water and assess the possibilities.

The river is only about 10 miles long; its source is the Chaba Glacier. We were at the midpoint of its length before it flows into the Athabasca River.

After almost two days of mosquito bogs, scary log bridges, and a long, swinging suspension bridge, our destination was in sight, just an icy, fast-flowing glacial river away. We had made it to the last channel of the river's braids.

I had first discovered this route over the Canadian Rockies while reading books about fur trader and map maker David Thompson. It is a low, gentle pass over the divide with Fortress Lake to the west, flowing into the Columbia by way of the Wood River. The Chaba flows past on the east into the Arctic Ocean via the Athabasca and Mackenzie rivers.

I felt drawn to this site immediately, and mysteriously, but did not want to go alone. So first I sold my wife, Linda, on the idea and then had talked to several friends who I thought would enjoy the trek. After planning for several months, I had five other adventuring souls who agreed to join me. All of us were excited about the quest.

We hit the trail at Sunwapta Falls, about forty minutes south of Jasper, Alberta. The falls at Sunwapta drop about sixty feet through a slot in the rock only thirty feet wide. We crossed over on a foot bridge and once we cleared the safety fencing we were on our way deep into Jasper National Park and its wilderness.

Our first day included a close encounter with a big Black bear who stepped out of the brush only a few feet ahead of us. He had been in a pond along the river we were skirting. A quick look in our direction and he dug his claws into the surface, scooping out divots in the trail, as he headed the other way. Pebbles zinged back toward us while he accelerated to full speed. His direction and urgency were just fine.

A good part of the day our trail was in the forest with filtered views of the Athabasca River and the craggy peaks towering over it. It crossed dark bogs where a toll was paid with blood; each one seemed to be a major population center for mosquitoes. We paid dearly as we hurried through.

The first day proved to be a little ambitious; we did nine miles. Arriving at our campsite, we were tired. Dropping our heavy packs lifted our spirits and lightened the load on our bodies. Shoulders, torsos, legs and feet relaxed after the long walk. We all sat and talked about the day, agreeing, even with some aches, we were very much up for the task we had embarked upon.

After setting up camp, we walked the couple hundred yards to the Athabasca Crossing foot bridge. It would be our first test of the second day. About two hundred feet long, it is suspended by heavy cables with a plank deck just wide enough to walk on. We all crossed over and back and felt confident that, with packs, we would do just fine.

After our first night sleeping on the ground we did the crossing and headed over a low ridge into the Chaba Valley. There were a few wood bridges to cross, some rather slippery, but we moved on, gaining confidence. About an hour before we reached the river I rounded a bend to see a stream fourteen feet wide, too deep to see bottom and flowing fast. Over it was a log—wet, slippery and appearing to be partially rotted. Andrew, a very experienced back country hiker, headed over first, sidestepping as he went; I was surprised the log didn't seem to sag under his weight. I knew there were some who would be apprehensive so I followed Andrew.

"Focus on the log, not the water," I said both to myself and the others.

Each moved slowly, using their poles with every step.

Narrow, slick, high passageways requiring excellent balance was a dragon in some of our minds. Everyone took a deep breath and moved across, slaying some of those dragons as we went. An hour later the trail delivered us to the wide open, flat bottom of the Chaba Valley, a grand reward.

I understand Chaba is native for Beaver, but we didn't see any sign of them.

It was early afternoon on that second day when we were standing in the middle of the stream. Jim, Andrew, Terry and I decided to wait and see if the river would be any lower the next morning. Glacial streams tend to flow lighter early in the day, before the ice starts melting. We headed back across the braids. Easy flowing streams cut narrow temporary rivulets in the gravely sand that separated us from the shore. Each one, between ankle and knee deep, reminded us this water had been ice recently.

Walking back to Linda and Michelle I wondered aloud if they would have a hot meal waiting for us. Terry asked what culture I thought I was living in. We laughed and I tried to make them promise not to repeat what I said. They said nothing; it was obvious there was no intention of making that promise.

It was in mid afternoon when we made camp and relaxed. Linda and I wandered around the valley a bit—wow! We were in an alpine meadow surrounded by serene, ice-capped peaks. It was easily a destination on its own, even if we did not ford the river. The bottom is a level floodplain with only short brush and grass. There were only a few trees so we could see the glacier-laden mountains around us without obstruction.

Our elevation was about 4,400 feet and directly across from us was Fortress Mountain. It is nearly shear from the bottom of the valley floor to its twin crags at roughly 10,000 feet. Behind was Quincy Peak, 10,000 feet with glaciers of blue ice framed by a hanging valley carved into the stone face. There was Sadler, just under ten, Chisel, over ten, Black Friar, over ten, Confederation, about eleven. We could not find names for three mountains within our view, each with its own rugged, ice-scraped beauty.

Up the river was Chaba Mountain, its ice cap piercing the sky, part of the Columbia ice fields and the source of the river. Down river to the north is Dragon Peak; we would camp across from it on our last night. Dragon Creek flows from snow and ice on this spire into the Athabasca. From beginning to end it looks like it travels as many feet vertically as it does horizontally.

We looked over the river to the pass that had been our goal for the hike. Sitting between Fortress and Sadler, which are only a couple miles apart peak to peak, the pass drops to its rounded base at less than half their height, creating an ice-rimmed basin falling off to the west.

Back in camp with the others, Jim, a hiker with many miles on his boots who can turn any event into a fun social occasion, walked in with a sly smile and sat down. With him were two water bottles he had been chilling in the river.

"I have margaritas," he said.

He had just assured his invitation to all future hikes I organize.

We built a fire and enjoyed our views and time together. Terry and Michelle were getting married in a few weeks, and we decided the wedding veil needed to be mosquito netting. Terry said when asked if he will take her as his wife he would answer, "In DEET I do."

As we slept it rained, all night and into the morning. Rain on a glacier is not conducive to lowering river flows.

Our time was short and we had to make a choice: stay put or try to get a glimpse of Fortress Lake. We chose to stay put - to just be. I felt some concern the others would be disappointed. Yet each one understood the wonderful journey we were on and accepted the change.

Once again, I was reminded it is the journey, not the destination, which is the goal. Is that the mystery I needed to solve?

We didn't want to rush out of the Chaba Valley. It would be a three mile hike back to the camp at Athabasca Crossing so we hung out until mid afternoon before we packed up and prepared for the walk out. We kept looking back and across rivers to the summits that had invited us and served as our magnificent, mountainous hosts.

We were six friends, each one with their own motivations for this quest. Each one chose to challenge themselves in this wilderness, a wilderness as beautiful as it is intimidating, as dramatic as it is peaceful. An individual and a shared adventure, just as each mountain and valley is separate yet part of the whole. We learned about dependence and independence and how we need both.

After bathing in the Spirit of the mountains we were back at the trailhead by mid-afternoon of the fifth day. With nearly thirty miles on our boots there were some blisters, some sore muscles and more than a few mosquito bites. We had fulfilled dreams, slayed dragons, and acquired many memories, all the while deepening relationships.

A nearly full moon was creating some wonderful moon shadows, both bright and mysterious.

Trusting Divine Intention

Fear was consuming me. I needed to prepare a talk for the next day, but nothing could get past the dam of fear that was dominating my thoughts.

In an attempt to deal with the developing affects of trepidation, the idea of setting an intention and being open and receptive to any, and all, divine ideas coming to me was obvious. However, I had to work past my uncertainties.

My home at the time was a cabin on a small mountain lake with wetlands just to the east; a shelter on a hill behind the house gave me the option of sitting out of the wind, rain, or hot sun, to meditate.

On that evening it seemed like a good place to do some "work" with Spirit. So with a small notebook and pen I headed up the trail.

There was a chair in this sanctuary but that evening sitting on the ground, being in contact with the earth, felt right. Glacier, a white German Shepherd, companion and roommate, lay beside me.

I thanked Spirit for the inspiration I was about to receive. I also repeated, "I'm open and receptive to all of God's goodness and grace," several times, then added, "I am filled with love; there is no room for fear." That affirmation put focus on good instead of apprehension. Sitting there I released the doubts and tried to be open to ideas of Spirit as they flowed through me.

It was comfortably warm in my light shirt as the dark was starting to creep into the valley. A nearly full moon was creating some wonderful moon shadows, both bright and mysterious, around us. Below, at the water's edge, a beaver was breaking the silence by gnawing on a willow. Out in the wetlands geese and their goslings were talking loudly to each other as they prepared to find a safe place to spend the night. The whistling of a merganser's wings close to the water passed.

The beaver chewed and rustled the brush at the water's edge until a branch fell into the water with a splash. Soon a wave spread across the lunar reflection, breaking it into bouncing fragments of light as the foliage was pushed toward the lodge.

The geese were starting to get quiet.

A deer nearby apparently smelled us for the first time and started snorting and stamping its hooves, hoping to chase us away. Both Glacier and I just let it have its little rant and continued to be quiet.

A coyote yipped on the hill high behind us as the forest darkened.

Getting a little stiff from the ground, I climbed into the chair.

I settled in, head resting against the back, repeating a mantra expecting to stimulate creativity. "Thank you for the wise words. Thank you for the good ideas. Thank you for the inspiration."

Glacier started to snore as I continued to calm my thoughts and moved into a meditation ready to receive godlike brilliance.

For some reason, maybe a noise in the woods, I suddenly woke up. The moon was gone, it was completely dark, and I was cold. Getting up out of the shelter I accidentally kicked the dog, who could not be seen in the lack of light. We started down the trail to the house without the assistance of any flashlight; root after root reached up and grabbed one foot, then the other. I stumbled and bounced off a tree.

It was very late, the middle of the night. In a few short hours I was going to be in front of a group of people giving a talk. I had no idea what I was going to say, or even a subject to talk about.

Freaking out due to my current state of affairs, I chastised myself. Why did I let this happen? Why didn't I just sit down and force myself to write? Why didn't I focus on the task at hand?

Somewhere between breaking the grasp of a root, tripping over Glacier again, and hitting another tree I hadn't seen, it came to me, a true moment of divine inspiration. "This is it, this is the talk."

When I saw what was happening I started to laugh. It was a great and funny story of putting faith in the wrong place, a perfect example of what "not" to do.

What I had done, after waking up, was immediately allow myself to be filled with fear because of falling asleep instead of preparing. I had set an expectation but wanted it to look differently than the one I received. I did not recognize it so went directly into panic. My belief is that when I am called to a task, the intention of the universe is I will complete that task; therefore I will be supported. But I put my faith in the fact that I still did not have a talk rather than trust all was in divine order. I only saw my inadequate preparation instead of the truth. When I caved to the

49

fear, that fear consumed me to the point of terror. I completely forgot what I had asked for when I had originally set my intention.

My talk was the story of my experience during the night, a perfect story about faith and intention and where to place it, or not.

Once I was in the cabin I fell into a restful sleep, knowing I had a talk for later in the day.

I still haven't found that notebook I had left in the dark forest.

A Community in the Woods

The call came mid-morning one day last summer from Tim.

"Ernie do you have someone visiting with a little girl about 9 years old?"

"No, why?"

"A little girl just showed up at Richard's and she said her dad and mom are in a log house. She doesn't know where."

We live in a community, or neighborhood, that isn't typical. From our house, we can't see anyone's lights. There is only one neighbor past our place so we rarely have traffic and when there is, we nearly always know them. Only the loudest noises of those nearest us get through the woods to squeeze the silence out of our serenity. Yet there are many folks up here.

I know several people who live in this kind of community and most of them say they wouldn't live any other way. They also say the community may look and feel loosely connected; however, it is tight-knit and dependable.

Tight-knit doesn't mean we are close, or there is a great deal of socializing within the group. There is some, but not a lot.

Yet when the call came that a girl had wandered out of the woods I knew it was a call to action and I was going to see several people I normally only wave to on the road. I only know the first names of most of them. In fact, some I see so rarely I hoped I would remember even that much, yet most of us have exchanged phone numbers for this very reason.

I called Terry right away but found no clues.

There is an old cabin deep behind us owned by an out-of-state family. They, or relatives of theirs, use it occasionally. When I drove there it looked like someone might be visiting, but I saw no cars and I couldn't raise anyone.

I headed out onto the main county road. There, I found vehicles of every kind: trucks, tractors, cars, ATVs, bicycles and one lady on a horse. Claire said someone was working on the

51

Wilson's log house. Jack said he would check it out, see if the girl belonged there.

Richard had called Grace immediately after the girl wandered out of the woods and she came right over. Grace and another neighbor rode up on four-wheelers with her. She was a stranger to us all. She did know her dad's name. Unfortunately, no one recognized it. With tears making rivulets in the dust on her face, she said she had been walking on a path in the woods but it all looked different now.

I told them it looked like someone might be back at the old cabin but I didn't see anyone. Grace mentioned an old logging road crossing the back of her place and close to Richard's house; it runs on through the woods close to the old cabin and might be the path in question. She was pretty sure, if someone had a chain saw handy, she could get through on an ATV quickly.

A cell phone rang and we heard there was a car with out-of-state plates on the back roads over the hill; someone headed that way to see if they had lost a kid.

Grace and a couple others, armed with a chain saw from a toolbox in the back of a truck, left with the girl on the ATV. The crowd seemed to have a few plans now to follow. I headed back toward the old cabin by road, just in case no one was there when Grace arrived.

As I approached the cabin I heard a chain saw in the distance behind it. "It must have been tougher going than expected," I thought.

This time, a rig with out-of-state plates was there. A lady came out of the cabin. I asked if they had lost a little girl. She was a bit frantic and said yes, had I seen her? Just then a man came out of the woods showing a controlled father's concern and said he thought they should call Search and Rescue. I said I think she's with the people using that chain saw we are hearing and she'll be here soon.

I asked his name; he gave me the same one the child said belonged to her dad. The mom said she had been driving around on the old roads thinking the girl wouldn't go into the woods.

I called Tim and told him the out-of-state car belonged to the old cabin and I was there with the parents. He asked if Grace was there yet.

"I can hear them close, must have more blow downs than she thought."

The noise from the saw stopped. The man headed toward the sound just as the ATVs appeared. When I saw them together, there was no doubt in my mind this was a family.

In less than an hour over 20 people literally "came out of the woods" to help a lost little girl.

Our neighborhood may not be typical yet I bet there are many just like ours where the same kind of action would take place, and just as rapidly.

Not many folks really live "outside" community any more. Some of us have moved, or stayed out of town because we want the space. We need the solitude of morning coffee on the porch hearing nothing but birds, watching the animals of the forest. We need a place where the lights of the city, or our nearest neighbors, can't be seen. We need a place where the traffic is rare and familiar.

Yet community is exactly what we have. We can depend on those nearest us to support each other when necessary, even though we are not socially connected. Many of the people I saw on the road that day I hadn't seen for several weeks—maybe months— and didn't see them again for months, yet we all came together when there appeared to be a need.

Sometimes, as I listen to the silence of our woods and watch the wildlife through the filter of the trees, I like to think we are in a wilderness alone, self-sufficient. In truth, I could not survive that way and really, I don't want to. I need and enjoy community.

Several breaks in the trees allowed for good picture taking of the Cabinet Mountains.

The Gift of Another Wonderful Day

On the south side of the trail was a small cedar grove, dark and delightful. The ground was covered with little vegetation other than the giant trees. Their branches touched each other high above the floor, creating a canopy the sun could not penetrate. As with nearly every shadowy, damp, musty valley filled with mature cedars, it had an enchanting, even mystical feeling. The shady path took Linda and I to the top of a rise; another similarly enthralling draw lay to our north. This was a temporary moment at the beginning of a new walk for us. In a short, pleasant, cedar-shaded saunter, we crossed a slight ridge and a vista opened to the east.

Several hundred feet below we could see Pend Oreille Lake and our destination, Evans Landing; in between was a steep, probably sixty percent grade.

55

We had talked about this trail, just a few miles from our home, several times. Looking at maps, we knew we would be traversing the nearly vertical west wall of the lake that runs from Maiden Rock south to Cape Horn.

What we had not researched was the trail itself. We tend to go into areas with the attitude. "If it gets too tough we will turn around." Like most people with that mind-set, we never have turned around. Would this be the first time?

Still, we were rather philosophical about it as we stood at the top looking down at the water below, then across and up to snow-covered Pack Saddle Mountain. She reaches up over 6,200 feet, more than 4,000 feet above the lake. We knew this view already made the day a success. However, the trek from this scene to our intended destination was still an unknown, yet inviting adventure.

Evans Landing is a narrow gravel beach on the west side of Pend Oreille. Mixed with the clean washed gravel are large, bluish-green bedrock boulders with deep, rutty glacial scars thousands of years old. For years, I had heard it was only accessible by boat, sometimes with the caveat, "Well, I guess there is a trail up the cliff but...."

I had boated in to the little bay a few times, tied to the mooring buoys and spend the night, but I had never gone ashore. Some people beach their crafts and camp, taking advantage of a couple fire pits and picnic tables.

Therefore, with only this limited knowledge, we started down the track leading to the beach.

As it opened to an eastern exposure, the forest changed from cedar and hemlock to mostly Douglas fir and some pine with a mix of birch. Low growing brush covered the ground, as more light reached the soil; still, there was plenty of shade from the morning sun.

Most hikers will tell you a downhill is harder on the body than a climb, especially on the knees. Fortunately, for most day hikes the morning is a climb with the day ending with a descent. It allows the ailing knees to sit down for the ride home followed by relaxing in a hot tub with a glass of wine in the evening. However, on this day we started with the downhill. I wondered how it would be getting back up. But, a little time pondering that, and I realized I was losing a wonderful trip worrying about something that might not happen.

We followed a gentle slope crossing the top of the face. The first switchback came after a rather long grade with several openings for viewing the west end of the Green Monarchs on the opposite side of the lake. All the switchbacks were long, making the slope very bearable and several breaks in the trees allowed for good picture taking of the Cabinet Mountains to the northeast.

We could have made good time but one thing kept slowing our progress; all the new spring flowers and plants. They ran the color gamut, from light pink to vivid purple and with textures ranging from white lace to brilliant yellow sunbursts all nesting in every hue of green. When we first spotted a Western tanager sitting in an Ocean Spray bush—with red head, yellow body and black wings—he looked like another flower, until he started flitting about.

Closer to the bottom, Maiden Rock could be seen protruding into the west shoreline a mile or so to the north.

The trail was narrow but never washed out and, to our surprise, was never excessively steep.

That is, until we were at the bottom. That is when I could understand the ominous stories I had heard of the trail "up the cliff." The last twenty feet or so to the beach was, basically, no trail at all. Still, we scrambled down it after doing a little study of the options. Really, it was only bad by the standard that had been set by a thousand or so feet of descent getting to it.

On the beach, we ate our snacks at one of the picnic tables as weather was rolling in over Bernard Peak and around Cape

Horn to the south. There was a little breeze making five- or six-inch waves lap at the shore, giving us perfect lakeside music.

From beach level, it was almost impossible to find the trail we had just come down. We had fun exploring the best route back up that first twenty feet; once past it the ascent was pleasant, even with a moderate sweat index.

One thing that added to the fun was the new pair of trekking poles gifted to me a few days before the hike. I had used ski poles adjusted for walking several times and knew how much easier they can make both ascents and descents. These new ones with cushioned handles and straps and breakaway tips were nicer.

I don't know how far the hike was in miles, but it took us a little over two hours each way at our leisurely pace.

As we reached the top, we stopped near the cedar groves we passed through earlier and sat down to meditate.

With a feeling of exhilaration, I remembered our early apprehension about the difficulty of the trail, and gave thanks for the reminder that perceptions can keep us from our goals.

I thanked the magnificent trees that shaded us, the views that pleased us, and the earth, who gave us this wonderful hill. I thanked those who came before and made the trail and finally Great Spirit for it all, and the gift of another wonderful day.

Just as we loaded into the car, that weather we had seen coming started pouring a drenching spring rain—thanks also for waiting just a few minutes.

She stopped and nuzzled the little one

Keeping Honest With …

I must admit a bias against elitism. With that disclaimer I still heard myself say, while driving into Yellowstone Park, "I don't want pictures of male deer, elk, or moose. I'll wait until their racks are fully grown."

We were wrapping up a road trip back from Virginia and spending a little time in the park before heading home. Linda, at the wheel, asked if she should even stop if we saw something. "Let's take a look, but probably not."

"What about bear?"

"This early in the spring and being on the main road, pretty unlikely."

"Babies?"

"We won't see them from the road this early, maybe some buffalo but that's about it. This will be a landscape day and the light looks to be pretty good for that, too."

So as the early morning sun climbed over the mountains

59

and backlit the mysterious mists of Yellowstone, we drove into a glorious day of picture taking. The clouds rising from the paint pots and hot mud created a spiritual sense as we started our adventure.

A car had stopped and was looking at a cow elk feeding on grass.

"Want to stop for a photo op?" Linda asked as she maneuvered around the car.

"No, I don't need another shot of a cow. If she had a calf I would, but that isn't going to happen from this road. Maybe I'll come back in the fall and see if there are any bulls with full racks."

"Well, aren't you the elitist photographer."

She does keep me honest, but still I didn't want to stop. I knew today was a good day to get those interesting Yellowstone photos, taking advantage of the early light.

Near a steam-shrouded river a herd of buffalo grazed. I got a few good shots.

"See, you get wildlife from this road," came a voice from the driver's seat.

"Okay, some buffalo maybe, but a car doesn't threaten them."

Then she said, "You know, they are really bison and not buffalo."

I thought to myself, "So who is being elitist now?"

A quick check on the iPhone proved her right. However, I almost got a point since "American Buffalo" was first recorded in the 1630s and the scientific name bison wasn't given until the 1790s.

If that had been right what would we call Buffalo Bill Cody? Don't forget the football team the Buffalo Bills; should they be the Bison Bills? Sounds like a big, overweight shaggy animal that stands around and lets you take its picture. Not exactly dramatic or intimidating, is it? I also knew I would get the last word because I was going to write the story.

As we followed the big, shaggy bison down the road, at less than two miles an hour, one mama stopped right in front of us and started nursing her baby. I asked, as we waited, if that was a mama bison or mama buffalo?

Linda said, "It doesn't matter. When there is a hungry baby, she is just a mama."

So I recorded some images of "buffalo" and some calves in their brown, baby coats, admitting quietly—very quietly to myself—she was right. A little later we were stopped again by a herd on the road. One made us wait as it left a sample of "buffalo chips" on the center line.

At Gibbon Falls, where the Gibbon River drops into the caldera, we watched and recorded the sun squeezing shadows out of the canyon. At Victoria Cascade the water looked to be flowing over the back of a steeply held cheese grater for several hundred yards. It was a good day to snap the shutter, even if the wildlife chances were slim to none in my mind.

As the road wove through a mountain meadow above a steep valley lined with deep green spring grass, several vehicles clogged the way. People with camera phones halted all travel. Looking for the interest, I got out.

Deep in the valley were a couple of Black Bear too far away to get a good shot with my telephoto lens. I snapped off one anyway and looked. All I had was two black spots, that with some imagination, looked like bears. I got a little testy listening to folks sound like great hunters closing in on prey. There wasn't a shot there with anything less than a thousand millimeter lens. I couldn't understand all the excitement.

Linda pointed out that these people probably don't have bear in their yard each summer as we do; this might be the only time they will get to see bears in the wild. Again, she managed to keep me honest.

By the time we were through the traffic jam the sun was getting higher and hot, and soon the light for pictures would be getting flat. We found a side road with not much traffic; it took us along a steep, treed hill on the left. On the right was a grassy opening with downed, gray weathered logs and marshes. The hills and forest made the light a little more interesting. As pretty and refreshing as the place was, there were no real photos.

We talked about the trip we had been on and this beautiful valley. There were some deer to watch but too far for a shot. A turkey vulture caught an early thermal and spiraled up looking for breakfast. We came into an area where a few trees stood between us and the opening. A movement caught my eye: another cow elk very near the road. She turned a little and took a step which revealed a very young calf.

Linda hadn't seen her. I pointed and she slowed to a stop. To my surprise the two of them were moving parallel to us with the calf between me and its mother—good shots. Sitting in the pickup I could shoot out the window, maybe that is why she stayed. She stopped and nuzzled the little one, splashed slowly through a marsh, then moved toward us and crossed the track close to our bumper. As she did Linda thanked her for giving us some time with her newborn, then they were gone.

We headed toward Mammoth and home. As we wrapped up the trip we talked about how expectations or our judgments of them can be so inaccurate. We were in one of the natural wonders of the world and I was trying to limit the experience by pointing out what I thought we would see. At the same time I was limiting the events of others, who were thrilled at their find. I take offence when that is done to me. It was time for me get honest.

In the end we saw wonderful landscapes, falls, geysers and steaming bubbling mud pots. There were bear, elk with a baby and, don't forget, the buffalo.

The surf has hammered these rocks into a tortured, distressed looking, eerie, weird shapes.

An Ever-Changing Constant

The boardwalk was mossy green planks, slick in places, but they kept us out of the muck below. The canopy of the old growth rainforest allowed minimal sun to dry the ground, so the alder, spruce, and cedars were gnarled and twisted, sometimes around themselves, sometimes around another tree, as they reached for light.

We were on the trail to Shi Shi Beach through the Makah Indian Reservation. Nearly the entire trail is in the Reservation, but the beach, our destination, was part of the Olympic National Park.

We walked on, in the damp, late afternoon dim of the woods.

Earlier, at the visitor center, purchasing park permits, we met the ranger.

"There are rules. You may not like them or even think they are right, but there are rules," he told us.

Most of the rules were typical of wilderness or national park hiking but there were a few additions

"You can build fires on the beach but not one big enough to be seen from another solar system.

"All food, garbage, or any scented items must be stored in bear canisters. This is because of raccoons not bears, food hanging in bags will be torn open and eaten.

"Finally," he said, "drive to the trailhead and drop your pack, then drive back along the road where you passed some houses with several cars in their yards and a cardboard sign saying 'park here.' Pay their price—whatever it is—and leave your car there. If you leave your car at the trailhead it will be gone."

"Do you mean towed?"

"No, gone. You are going into another country; this is like Ecuador in the 1970s. Pay their price to park in their yard, it will be fine there."

The trailhead parking lot sign said, "For Overnight Parking Use Secure Lots."

So we dropped our gear and drove back, where we found a steel box to put our money. There was a sign above it at read: "Ten dollars for the day you arrive, no matter how late. Ten dollars for each day your car is here, and ten dollars for the day you leave, no matter how early." That price was paid—after we found some journal paper to wrap our money in.

The ranger had said, "They do not invest your money on signage, striping or envelopes." He seemed to be right.

Appreciative and entertained by the presentation, we followed all the rules to the letter. Although we did notice the only thing secure in the secure parking area was the steel box where we left our money.

We had done some research before the trip, so we knew the boardwalk would end before the mud bog did and we were ready for a slog. It wasn't as soggy as expected. Our boots got covered and our pant legs dirty, but it was not nearly as bad as we understood it could be.

Just before entering the park there are some openings in the forest. A hundred or so feet below each one lay the Pacific Ocean, with scattered rocky outcroppings. Small to huge free-form, sculptured islands dotted the sand and the surf. White foam slammed against them so hard you would think they would move, but the wave was broken instead.

A steep trail down the cliff had to be negotiated before reaching the beach. We had heard it was very treacherous and a rope was provided for the descent. On our day it was not as slippery as expected but still, many countless roots made the dirt track a challenge; not at all insurmountable, but challenging just the same.

At the bottom, the trail headed toward the beach past a privy with a single "modesty" panel that could be seen over and around— I guess it was better than digging a hole.

Shi Shi Beach is a long, sandy, rock-strewn coastline. At the north is a rocky headland and the two-mile-long shoreline runs south to another: the Point of Arches.

We set up camp at the demarcation where the rain forest spilled down the cliff to join the light brown sand.

A hike to the north headland allowed close inspection of the rocks.

Conglomerate rocks are sandstone working like a mortar for larger stones and boulders of different kinds and sizes called clastics. They have been pressed into a hard sarsen, looking a little like a large aggregate and concrete mix.

For millennia, the surf has hammered these rocks into a tortured, distressed look—eerie, weird shapes looking structurally unsound, but standing strong against the ocean's power.

Around and between them are motes and wonder-filled, small tide pools, teaming a with diversity of life and color. Bright orange, to burgundy, to purple, to neon violet, starfish wait to catch a ride on the next tide.

At one point we kept hearing a recurring boom. A search led us to a small cave where the waves trapped and compressed air until the power of nature blasted, blowing vapor back out the opening.

Early the first morning I experienced a karmic moment. On the horizon we saw the spray of whales. The spray was all we could see at first, yet I felt elation in the occasion. Then I remembered a few weeks earlier in Yellowstone Park, I had become cranky when tourists clogged the road looking at bears several hundred yards away. It was not a bear sighting, only a "couple of black dots" sighting. Now I was acting the same as those people each time I saw a spout in the distance. I got it: we can all get excited about witnessing something we are not used to seeing.

Finally, one of the giant mammals seemed to lie at the surface for a while. As I watched with binoculars it dove, giving a great show of flukes high out of the water followed by a massive splash. During that day we saw otters, and seals, cavorting near the shore while eagles glided over us into the trees.

The days were spent hiking the beach, sometimes barefoot, connecting to the ocean as an ever-changing constant. It is a force that may appear destructive yet, it is the reason for the wonderful, irregular rocks and beach where we camped.

On the fourth day we walked the trail back through the Reservation to the lot where we had left the cars. Just as before there were no lines, no permanent signs, and no one—and the cars were not gone.

Walking from peak to peak stressed both lungs and legs

Trusting to See What is Needed

The hill was steep, but not exceptional, and I had only hiked about a mile, yet still my lungs felt like I was sucking air through a small twisted straw. The burn in my legs, even at the slow pace I was setting, was all too real. In fact, pace sounds a little too much like progress, it was more a "walk a while and stop" routine. Each stop allowed for views across deep and steep valleys to other ridges and peaks. A glorious place and a glorious day with gorges dropping abruptly from the trail to tiny unnamed lakes and ponds, giving me the feeling of being on top the world.

Wait a minute, on top of the world? That was it; the trailhead was nearly six thousand feet high, an elevation where I usually end my hikes, or turn around and start back down. No wonder my lungs wheezed and my thighs hurt.

This was Stag Leap Provincial Park where the trails begin at the top of the pass and go up. It is an easy drive from home, in fact a good day trip, though I planned for more.

The morning drive north with the sun coming over the

Cabinet Mountains and shining onto the Selkirks was exquisite. To my surprise though, the high point of the day, so far, was not the Purcell Trench in the morning I was driving through, rather, a cinnamon roll found in a small general store and bakery a few miles north of Bonners Ferry. It was world class. The first one I have found I could not finish in one sitting. Not because it was too big, I've had bigger. It was just too darn rich and sweet.

I didn't believe it was possible – neither did my wife when I called and told her. For her, when it comes to sugary goodies, a dip of her finger in the frosting is enough. However, I am quite good at eating super sweet stuff. Ironically, as I was heading for the mountains of Canada, I found a sweet treat peak I could not scale on the first attempt. I savored the surprise as I drove north with half a bakery delicacy on the seat beside me.

Reaching Kootenai Pass in early afternoon, some close in exploring was in order. Wandering around Bridal Lake and then back along the Bear Grass trail via Cornice Ridge, I figured out what the agenda would be tomorrow. There were several more trails needing my footprints.

Back in the car and driving down the west side of the pass, the valley spread out with mountain splendor rarely found on a major highway. Needing a spot to spend the night away from the noise of the road I turned onto a single-track lane, which took me to the Salmo River, a perfect spot. The river's song covered the growling of the trucks up and down the pass and gave it a wilderness feel.

I was in an opening where the river flowed directly to me then turned just below my campsite. I could see where the water had been gnawing away at the bank for centuries. In a few more this site would erode completely.

On the valley walls, and floor, the golden tops of aspen and birches reached out from between the Sub Alpine firs, glowing in the waning light. Fall was in the dale.

Someone once said, and I have used it on several occasions

in different seasons, "If there is a time of year to just stop and absorb the beauty of all that surrounds you...it's now."

I love finding places like this, especially when I don't have a plan.

The next morning, while having coffee on a rock next to the river and finishing the pastry from the day before, I found a conflict struggling within me. I didn't want leave this serene setting and I wanted to be back up trekking above the pass. Knowing the ridges would wait made it easy to settle in on a stream side log for a long morning meditation. The feeling of the mountain energy, carried by the water to my camp in the valley, was my reward.

At mid morning I was on the trails; up was the only way to go.

It was just off the main trail when I had the realization I was not used to hiking at these altitudes. Yet I loved every step, each one higher than the last. The trail became less evident so I followed the rim between two canyons; still I didn't feel I was the first there.

The next bombshell discovery, maybe literally, was a sign bolted to a tree. It was bright red and yellow with black block lettering, the obvious product of a professional.

"Danger, avalanche control explosives may begin without warning."

I had been thinking of coming back later to do some snowshoeing. The warning nipped that plan in the bud. Next was a structure I still don't understand with another sign. "If you find deformed, or unexploded shells, contact the Ministry of Transportation." So, rather than scanning the vistas of cliffs and peaks to the horizon I was looking at the ground like a soldier in a minefield.

I had been out of the trees for quite a while so nearly all the vegetation was less than knee high. With each step, the pebbles under my boots moved a little giving a sound and feel of treading on a gravel walkway.

At the peak where the ridge ended, no unexploded shells had been seen. Looking beyond that point were more inviting ridges to follow, and higher, peaks to explore. Unable to resist, my trek took me to those narrow ridges. Walking from peak to peak stressed both lungs and legs. It also allowed wonderful views of deep narrow valleys where winter snows often hang in the shadows all summer.

I surveyed the grandeur while a brisk wind snapped the sleeves of my jacket like a flag on an antenna.

I thought about the pleasure I get from trips like this, with no real plans. The needs of the moment are revealed as necessary when I just trust my inner guidance.

Retracing my steps I reviewed the trip in my mind. It had been full of new and wonderful discoveries. New trails and ridges, a great campsite, and a cinnamon roll, all will need revisiting.

Back at the top of the first peak I looked down the hill and could almost see where I left the car, but I could not see where the trail entered the trees from my vantage.

A message came clear to me as I started back down. It was an old message but as usual, I had to climb to the top of a mountain to relearn it.

I could see where I wanted to be, but no clear path for getting there. I cannot let the inability to see the route keep me from my goals. In fact, there is no way for me to find the route unless I start. It forces me back to trust. I will see the way as I need it, but only when I move forward.

...forcing them to browse on the fruits of the forest, to find the wealth around them on their own

A Lesson Told by the Animals

A doe and her twins cautiously stepped out of the safety of the dense forest. Fresh, moist shoots of brush and new stalks on the low growing grass in the clearing were inviting delicacies after a long winter.

Knowing the danger of not having a stand for cover, she was wary, and looked vigilantly to her right. In her periphery a cougar leaped from the shadows. The mother made a swift turn to escape; her twins, white tails erect, shining an alarm, scattered into the shadows just as the cat grabbed at the doe's back. The deer's speed, and the low branches of fir trees in the dimness of thick woods, and brush, kept the big cat from getting a grasp of more than superficial flesh and the mountain lion was scraped to the ground. The doe continued her dash, running under branches and cutting sharply around undergrowth. The cougar had only a short sprint in the nearly impenetrable vegetation before it tired.

I sat quietly on my porch listening to the silence that so often fills our woods. It was one of those early spring days when industry seems to be everywhere - except in me. I watched the swallows winging about, bringing nesting material into a nearby box on a tree. Two juncos had discovered the remains from the last brushing of the dog and excitedly gathered it for a nest. A robin splashed in a puddle that was ice a few days earlier. I wondered how cold it must have been, but the birds seemed to enjoy it.

Branches on the conifers had shed their load of snow and were starting to reach up to the light again, as languid air currents moved them slightly and silently. The light of a fresh new day was making its way through the thick timber that surrounds the opening around our home.

Suddenly hooves were pounding on the earth, branches breaking and wood snapping, brush whipping and slapping, as an animal broke the silence with panic. My senses - sound, sight, and smell - came to complete attention as the aural discord of the morning approached.

Near the edge of our meadow the doe appeared, breathless, adrenaline pumping. Still wild eyed, she stopped; I had a filtered view of her through trees and leafless bushes, as she looked around, keeping in the protection until she felt the safety of our place. With binoculars, I watched the terror fade as she surveyed the opening, a familiar spot where she and the twins often drank from the wooden barrel and bedded down under the trees.

I recognized her by a small mark on her face as she stepped into the clearing, giving room to reach around and clean the fresh wound on her back.

Deep, but not mortal; she took care of it. I knew the cleaning would avoid infection and help eliminate odor that may expose her vulnerability; she simply knew to tend to it.

It appeared she also knew Spirit would let her offspring know where she had stopped and shortly, one bounced onto the work road to the west. The other came down a trail and moved in and out of view through the brush until it could start nursing.

The scene of the attack I imagined. It was based on the shape and location of the wound, the panic, and the need to rush through an extremely dense stand - all consistent with a cougar encounter. But I can only speculate that is what happened.

Many native cultures believe each animal species has its own medicine. This is not medicine as we traditionally define it, not a product that will heal or cover symptoms, but a life enhancement to help us understand the Great Mystery. Deer medicine is gentleness.

As I watch life in the wild, I struggle to be the observer without human emotion and judgment, taking away the story, leaving only the now.

Even so, I had watched this animal for years; I first saw those twins when they stood on shaky legs, I felt her fear and the fear of the babies, worried that the injury might become infected, even held anger for the cougar; put my judgment on it.

Watching her I was reminded of gentleness.

A slight breeze caused the bamboo wind chimes on the corner of the porch to start its clink-clinking music. Obsidian crystals hanging from the roof started to chinkle. There was a call to connect with Earth while pondering the lesson of Deer. I looked at her and asked, "Teach me your lesson."

Wanting to leave without disturbing the doe and fawns, I took a path in the opposite direction; Nikki, our dog, followed and we entered the forest. The breeze picked up a bit and sang a song of peace in the crowns of the trees. I tried listening but was not really at peace; I had a haunting concern about the deer, fear she might not be able to protect herself and the babies, and there was that anger for the cougar flowing in me.

Finally, sitting cross-legged under a large Ponderosa, Nikki stretched out in a Hemlock's shade, I began to calm my thoughts.

The leaves were budding on the Ocean Spray bush; the blossoms that give it its name would be appearing soon. The odor of last year's leaves and needles composting on the forest floor was all around. The tang of animals shedding their winter coats helped me center. The scent from aged stumps and logs torn open in the search of a meal, grounded me.

Asking for understanding I heard the gentle wind rustle the tops of the trees and experienced the energy of the earth. It helped slow my conflicted mind.

I listened to the flow of the wind interrupted by the branches; I could feel the power of the earth under me as I asked Great Spirit, "What is my lesson?"

Since Cougar had come into my mind it was as present to me as the deer. I knew in my heart not to be angry.

Cougar medicine is leadership; the ability to focus, hold an intention, to act at just the right time, the ability to look quickly at other options and to be flexible enough to change course with confidence. The lion of our woods is about balance; I admire all its characteristics and strive to practice them. The big cat is not a terrorist, but part of a greater design that can't be faulted. Or one I even could understand.

I heard, "look, observe without judgment, be only present."

Spirit spoke again into my consciousness, the lesson was not about the lives of the animals involved, or their conflicts. The fear and anger were my story. The story of the encounter was not Deer's story. She had told me her story; a mother with twins and a wound, that was it- the whole story.

How would I react if I had been hit like that? I'm afraid I would be boring anyone who would listen to the drama as often as I could.

Or, could I be Cougar and change my focus; not relive the story, so as not to keep dumping that negative energy and the toxins that accompany it into my systems? Could I be Deer, caring for myself by being vigilant with my thoughts in each moment, allowing me to be present, my fullest expression of my God self?

As an old snag moaned while it rubbed against a large tamarack I heard, "Am I boring people with wounds that are deep inside, hurts, gossips, ridicules and judgments about others which are, in truth, about me?"

I struggled to focus on my story, to see the wounds I carry.

A few weeks later it was a quiet day during the late summer, the kind of day we like to call "another brutal day in paradise." The grass was starting to dry and the blossoms of spring had turned into fruit. The twins were much bigger; soon their dappled, fawn coloring would give way to a brown-gray winter coat. The wound had closed on Deer's back and fur was starting to fill in where the flesh was once torn. She stepped away as the youngsters reached for a teat, gently forcing them to browse on the fruits of the forest, to find the wealth around them on their own.

With Nikki stretched beside me, I was cross-legged under the Ponderosa observing the early autumn woods. Once again Cougar appeared in my consciousness, a reminder to be aware of the course I had chosen. Was it still serving me, or was I charging in the wrong direction? Then Deer was in my mind as she browsed to sustain strength for life, hers and her twins, her only work.

The story became clear to me. Surprising there was no story at all. There was only a deer with twins and a wound, nothing more. I created the attack - even the cougar - in my attempt to put judgment on that wound. It's what I teach but needed to relearn; to be only the observer.

I thanked them both for the lessons and for the reminders and of the value of being present. To be the observer and not put my judgment on what I see.

We watched the sunrise over Koko crater with coffee, fresh pineapple and papaya.

Another Way to Spend Winter

I told my publisher, who is not fond of winter, I was going to write about the cold dark season.

Her response was, "Oooh, you're going to wax on and on about how wonderful winter, and snow, and ice, and cold are, right?"

I could do that. I do enjoy winter and everything it brings. I have said before I'm not sure if winter is my favorite season but it's in the top four.

However, I have discovered another way to cope with snow, and it came as a complete surprise to me. It is from a new teacher who I'm sure will have many more lessons for me. Most of them I don't even know I need to learn yet, but they will be clear when presented. The teacher is my new granddaughter, Alice Lindy, who was born three days before Christmas.

And the lesson she taught me about coping with snow; do it in Hawaii.

The Islands had never been high on our places to visit until a couple of years ago. The Navy told my stepdaughter and her husband their services were needed at Pearl Harbor. Well, at least Noah's services were needed so, of course, Ana moved there also.

Right away, we knew we would be vacationing there sometime during his tour. We were thinking of a fall trip before air fares spike for Christmas. It would also allow us to be home for winter fun and frolic.

Then last spring the call came, "Could you please come for Christmas, pleeease?"

"Well, okay, I guess if it's that important." We knew Noah would be on deployment so not able to celebrate with his wife.

"Good, you can be here when the baby arrives." Ana has a way of getting the family together for the holidays.

That is how Alice taught us a new way to cope with snow.

As soon as we heard the first grandbaby in the family was arriving, we knew our vacation in Hawaii would not necessarily be a tour of a tropical paradise, and that was fine with us. A newborn in the house would take most of the time and our vacation would be a wonderful experience of getting to know this new kid in town.

However, when the baby was about a week old, Linda and I did manage a couple of outings as Ana, with the help of friends, took care of Alice.

First, we did a fun hike on Aiea Ridge Trail. Not far from Honolulu city center, this is a state park with fantastic views of Halawa Valley. It is rather surreal to look down from a narrow mountain ridge into a jungle-filled gorge with a four-lane freeway (H3) entering the picture, top center, appearing out of a tunnel in the steep canyon wall. The wall is so steep the lanes ride a viaduct over a mile long before reachine the canyon floor.

Further along the trail we enjoyed southern views of the crater Diamond Head, as well as the many bays of Pearl Harbor, all backed by the South Pacific and blue skies with white cotton clouds for perfect accent.

For us, the real treat was the forest, or forests, on this tropical trail. As we moved up and down, changing elevations from about six hundred feet to nearly sixteen hundred, we passed through several different environments, each with its own kind of beauty.

I was surprised at the steep gorges dropping on both sides. In some we passed the lacy needles of the Ironwood trees; a little farther was a grove of naked-looking giant Eucalyptus trees. At one point a dense bamboo forest with tall shoots on both our left and right created walls like a hallway without a roof.

Another environment was grass, grass taller than Linda before it bent and reached back down to the ground. Aiea is an excellent few hours I would recommend to any hiker visiting Oahu.

On another day we actually left Ana and Alice to have their first overnight alone. Ana kept telling us we needed a Hawaii vacation.

Our friend Chris, who has lived on Oahu for three decades, had been after us for years to visit her, so we accepted her offer and spent a night in her waterfront home in Hawaii Kai. Chris is a gracious hostess, and like many islanders the most used room of her home is the lanai. We enjoyed dinner there and the next morning we watched the sunrise over Koko crater with coffee, fresh pineapple and papaya.

Later we hiked the Makapuu trail, the most eastern point on Oahu. It is an old paved road about two miles long, a constant climb. There is about a 450-foot elevation gain from the trailhead to the observation deck. The deck sits atop a 600-foot cliff that drops to vibrant blue water. Unlike Aiea, there is no shade; it is a separate environment on the same small island.

The ocean views were startlingly close. The lower section presented dramatic views into Koko crater and along the windward coast. As we climbed, we were awe struck by the many vivid shades of blue the ocean water showed us as it crashed on the rocks at the bottom of the cliffs just below us.

From the track, we watched humpback whales swimming the channel with Molokai in the hazy distance. Part way up we passed a lighthouse, built in 1909 and still in use. On top, we looked down on it, again with a backdrop of that rich ocean water.

It was a wonderful outing and when we met Ana, she and Alice were tired but just fine.

One of Alice's first outings was a drive up to the North Shore. The intention was to see that world famous winter North Shore surf. I found it impressive. I'm guessing the waves were over 10 feet, not real high by their standards but it looked like a huge wall of water to me.

While the baby was feeding in the car, Linda and I walked the beach. With cameras in hand, looking for the perfect wave to catch and photograph, we came upon two sea turtles sunning on the sand and more swimming off shore.

I have photographed several species of wildlife over the years. But, I found a Sea Turtle sunning in the sand the easiest wildlife photo op I have ever been given.

These guys were three to three-and-a-half feet long, and probably weighed around 400 pounds. An oddity on the North Shore is both males and females come ashore; in most places only the females crawl up on the sand.

Back at the car Alice was well fed and asleep and ready for the drive back into town.

So a little baby girl taught me another way to enjoy the cold dark season. Yes, I was glad to get back to our misty winter woods, but I bet there will be another vacation sometime on the Islands. Maybe even after Alice and her parents move back to the continent.

I wonder what Alice's next lesson is for me?

The sight, smell, feel, even taste of autumn fills my senses

Peace is an Inside Job

Peace of mind was not possible; the meditative music flowing from the brand new PC did not help. My patience for computers was not influenced one iota by the Paul Winter Concert and the soft soothing sounds being delivered through the Internet radio, even though the new system made my work space sound like a stone cathedral.

Each time the new software tried to help me or fix something I didn't want fixed, my frustrations grew.

After a while Enya was soothing my workspace with her sweet, clear voice and it sounded like I was sitting in a Scottish castle, but she wasn't bringing patience, either.

I use the tool daily, but at times, it torments me, so when my aggravation gauge starts spiking into the red zone, I bolt for our woods. As I bounded down the stairs from the loft where my desk is I heard R. Carlos Nakai playing his cedar flute with a string symphony behind him. But even he could not stop me.

Stepping out into fresh air was like an escape from the irritation I blamed on that contraption sitting in the office.

Just outside the door Nikki, our dog, was excited to see me.

81

Most dogs wag their tails, but Nikki just wags, all 90 pounds of her. In her presence, my mood lifted.

Still on the porch I felt a breeze brush across my face full of its own sounds of meditative music. There were variations from the wind chimes, scattered around our property. The bamboos singing harmony with the clink clinking of obsidian crystals while soft gongs of metal pipes filled out the lower clef from a nearby tree.

From the porch as we wandered down a forested trail; I listened to a different kind of wind-inspired music, the air currents singing as the crowns of trees redirected them. The crackling of drying grass under each step added rhythm to nature's orchestra.

The sight, smell, feel, even taste of autumn filled my senses, a reminder it was nearly time to embrace another season.

The stress of work began to fade out of me just as the green was fading out of the leaves of the Oregon grape bushes along the path.

Autumn is the season of shedding, and a time of peace.

Each day the sun's arc slightly lowers in the southern sky, making the forest shade a little darker.

Fledgling birds have started flying and feeding without assistance. I saw some fawns I had watched nurse a few weeks earlier browsing on the drying leaves and grass, gaining nourishment from the abundance around them.

In the woods, out of sight and sound of the computer, peace wafted through my mind, body and spirit. Why did I feel peace? I knew the apparatus in the house was still not going to respond any differently to my commands. Yet, I did start to feel peace.

Above me, a branch of a Grand fir was sliding back and forth along the trunk of an old snag, making a moaning sound like a bow on the strings of a contra bass.

I was one with the peace of the forest.

With Nikki lying in a hemlock's shadow and a chickadee on a branch singing its cavalier "chik-a-dee-dee-dee" song, I sat down against a fir tree.

Still wondering, "Why is peace in me now? Is it because I am in my woods?" That usually happens, but the woods have no power over my inner feelings.

Was the tree at my back giving me peace? It had wonderful energy but cannot control my thoughts.

The bird, as beautiful as it was, could not sing peace into me.

The earth where I sat cross-legged nourished my spirit as always, but even it could not lift peace into me.

The wind and all its wonderful music could not blow peace on, or through, me.

That is when I heard Spirit say, "I have to be willing to be at peace, if I want to be at peace."

Years ago, my understanding of peace became personal. I was experiencing severe pain. The pain hurt my body but not my mind, or some may say soul. I discovered that it was possible to be at peace, and treat those around me as I wanted to be treated, even when ordinary movement was uncomfortable - at times debilitating. I simply chose not to allow the suffering to have power over me.

My thoughts went back to those days of pain and my decision to find peace in it.

Then a rather distressing thought entered my consciousness, gently, like a butterfly landing on my shoulder, soft but very present. I heard I could have that same peace while working at the computer, even as I learned to understand the new systems.

Peace is not the absence of conflict. Within that conflict I can have an understanding of myself, an understanding that allows me to transcend what is around me. And around me is exactly where it is, not in me, unless I choose to let it be there.

At that moment I wanted to say, "No, that can't be. I don't want to be at peace with that computer, I don't like it."

However, if I can choose to be at peace in our timbered glen and if I can choose to be at peace with pain, why can't I choose to be at peace with the computer?

Fall is the season of shedding; the trees shed needles and branches, while the brush shed spent leaves. To be wholly present in the season of shedding maybe I, too, needed to look for what is unnecessary in my life. Was I holding onto an old attitude (peace comes from outside me or the computer can take my peace away) that was keeping me from my fullest potential? Was I accepting peace into all my life? Was I being who I came here to be?

I did buy all that new hardware and software to make my life better. Then I upgraded with all the bells and whistles to make my life better yet, even play beautiful music on it. That should have been all I need for peace - the latest and greatest computer.

However, the fir tree could not give me peace, the wind could not blow away distress, and the computer could not make me suffer… unless I allowed it.

Did that mean I could find peace in that expensive, sophisticated tool sitting on my desk? It would depend on how I choose to react to it or not react to it.

Nikki woke up, wagged over to my shade; she nudged me to continue our walk. I took a little more time to listen to the music of the forest, but I knew it was time to get back to work. Before moving, I gave a thank you to Nikki, to the wind, to the forest, to the trail, to the earth, and to Spirit for yet another lesson.

One way for me to be with peace is to be thankful. So I gave thanks while walking back along that forested trail lined with colored leaves about to be shed, and I made a quiet personal affirmation, to be open to the season of shedding and to the reminders of peace and permit it into all of my life.

Sitting down at the computer, I realized it too was part of that all. So, I gave thanks for the computer that had entered my life.

Turning on the meditative music, I prepare for a new beginning.

An Impermanent Life

As the storm raged, the big old stiff pine snag swayed violently from a mighty gust. Two bald eagles sitting high above the lake on bare, gnarled branches opened their wings and lifted into the air. With a deafening crack, another exposed rotting root broke and, with panicking ducks below on water scattering into the wind, the tall, gray weathered sentinel made a thunderous crash into the lake.

I had watched this standing dead tree for over thirty years; in fact, I named it The Eagle Tree because of so many sightings I had there. Over the years waves breaking at the roots washed away the soil and rocks that gave this grandfather of the forest its stability. Each year it seemed another dead branch shed and floated away. It was obvious the time was near for the majestic old fellow to lie down. The only disappointing part is I was not with it—I could only imagine how the final moments played out.

Walking around a bend in the trail I looked west a quarter of a mile to where I always saw The Eagle Tree, but not that morning. A few more steps and I saw its remaining branches sticking out of the water several feet from the shore. A Kingfisher, looking for breakfast, perched on one.

Sitting at the base of my old friend I couldn't help but think about the impermanence of all nature—of everything.

It was the first of June and as I was walking toward the old tree I had been thinking of Father's Day and specifically about Noah, our son-in-law, as this would be his first Father's Day as a dad.

I've known him for nearly ten years and have always liked him. When I heard he and Ana were "an item," I was pleased and it has been exciting watching them develop a loving relationship and marriage. Now there is a baby girl.

As expected, he has changed during those years, and with that, some attitudes have too. Often it is called maturing but what it means is things that were important are now set aside and he has a different focus. All of this growth has created a man who is intelligent, compassionate and disciplined.

He was at sea when his daughter, Alice, was born so they didn't meet until she was two months old. When I saw the pictures and videos of their first time together, I saw a father—a family man with a new and wonderful focus.

Speaking of discipline you should have seen him, as cameras flashed and the video rolled, trying to hold it together like a strong sailor as he came ashore. In his words, "I cried like a little girl."

A few weeks later, we met them in Seattle. They were vacationing and we joined them to celebrate his birthday and be with the family. This was our first time being with him and his daughter together. I'm biased, but I think he is one of the most engaged fathers I have been around - equally involved in every part of the baby's care

The first time I held that little girl she was only a few hours old. It may sound like a schmaltzy pop song but my heart opened up in a way it never had before and she crawled right in. I have seen the same has happened to Noah.

So as I was sitting next to The Eagle Tree I was thinking about impermanence and Father's Day. At first the two thoughts felt incongruent, but as I sat with them, they began to reconcile in my mind.

I have seen an attitude change in our culture. The expectations of the father of my youth are different in many ways from today. As a child I thought fatherhood meant providing for the family with food and shelter but not always being present in the family. Now fathers are more involved in the daily care of their children. The permanence of old attitudes has evolved into a new and much better norm.

When I think of Noah—all of us for that matter—I think about how perspectives change. As important as our ideas and beliefs were, they are not permanent either. Of course, that doesn't mean they were wrong at the time; they too evolved.

When I first met Noah, he was excited and proud, with good reason, of his hot new sports car. He told me about how fast it was, and how tight and flat it cornered. Today he drives an SUV; his needs have changed. His zest for life is very much intact, but like his ride, it takes a different form.

So, The Eagle Tree is down and the view along the trail is different, but I'm sure there is another standing dead Eagle Tree somewhere. I will find it and hope it's permanent enough to last for the next thirty years. If it isn't, I hope I can be there to see the storm that proves it, too, is impermanent.

One thing that is not impermanent is Alice's place in Noah's heart. However, even that will grow and evolve into a larger and more expressive form of love.

I had watched this standing dead tree for over thirty years; in fact, I named it The Eagle Tree.

A low heavy ceiling of clouds held the sun at bay and kept cleaning the area with rains

Over-the-Hill-Itis

Well, it looks like my sixty-first Thanksgiving and holiday season is upon us so it is time for that list of stuff I'm thankful for. First on the list is the fact that making lists is really boring, keeping a lot of folks from writing them; for that I'm thankful.

That pretty much takes care of my list for the year.

Another thing that happens each year at this time is birthdays for both my wife and I; for that I'm thankful.

Each year we try to go someplace just for us, someplace we both want to visit. This year we took a long weekend to the Swan Valley in Montana. Several years ago I rode my bicycle through there but Linda had never seen it. I was able to show her another beautiful place.

While there the low cloud cover hid the jagged peaks on each side of the valley, making the few breaks that exposed the 7,000-to nearly 10,000-foot mountains, which create the high horizon for both the sunrise and the sunset, even more dazzling.

Our plan had been to do several day hikes up the draws and over the hills at the foot of the mountains. However, we decided warm and dry was a better idea for this trip and let the Toyota do the hiking on Forest Service and logging roads for us. Still, we managed some close looks at the rocky, glacial-scraped faces of the peaks several hundred feet high. The pines, firs and larches cannot get a grip on many of the cliffs yet the narrow gorges in them left by the ice age provides excellent habitat for the forest just below.

It was in these tapered, nearly vertical-sided ravines that our track had been carved as we ascended to nearly five thousand feet. Even in the late fall, white water cascaded through the canyon floor below us.

When there were breaks in the haze, we had expansive views of snow-covered monoliths guarding the basin below. Moisture-laden fog clung to the sides, showing only the tops of the trees, giving the woods a gauzy sense of mystery. On the bottoms it lay like rumpled downy blankets giving a feather softness to the severe, dramatic geography of the area. I think, at the risk of sounding like a list, I can say I'm quite thankful for the mystery of the seasons that change continually - yet no season is ever repeated. Each year the mystery is renewed.

When Linda and I get out in situations like this, whether in the car or walking, we both get stricken by a syndrome we can't control. It has several names: often called over-the-hill-itis, or around-the-bend-itis. Some people who aren't real familiar with the condition may call it "too curious for your own good" or just "lack of common sense." Whatever you want to call it we often get a serious case of it and for that I'm thankful.

Earlier in the afternoon we had checked with some locals and read some maps and knew we were coming to a fork in the road. Our intention was to turn right and head on down the loop we were on toward the highway. When we arrived at the fork it was quite plain, well marked and confirmed right was the direction we needed to take. Then Linda looked up to the left and just above clouds saw a scar crossing a snow-covered meadow just below the tree line; for that I'm thankful.

"I wonder if this road goes up there?" At that moment there was no curing either one of us as we headed left up the grade into the fog in search of a fix.

Coming out of the fog we were looking west to the Mission Mountains. Between was Swan Valley and somewhere down there under the mist was the cabin we called home for the trip.

Due to the grade we were climbing each tire had to scramble for grip. One slipped, another would get a hold, so we moved forward and up slipping, gripping and grabbing over the red dirt earth until just before we started into snow when the earth turned gray. Another mystery we could not explain.

As the tree line neared the snow was tickling the underside of the SUV, but we continued to slip, grab, slide and grip to new horizons. One of us said (I really don't know who but we both heard it) "Did we bring tire chains?" I wasn't sure if they were still on board from last year, or not. This encouraged a decision to stop and make a lunch; looking to see if we had chains filtered into my consciousness also. So at a switchback we stopped for a bite and a look.

We had driven into a deep canyon reaching easterly close to the Bob Marshall Wilderness. On the other side of the chasm was a rock wall disfigured by chutes where avalanches had smoothed the surface and crashed down into the forests below, taking everything in their path. In each one a white ribbon of water, tumbling and free falling, dropped through them, allowing for the only sound we heard there that day.

We ate while appreciating where we were, then walked up the road a short distance. The sun was not visible but we knew it would be dropping behind the western wall of the Missions soon, taking any light we had with it. We both still had a nearly irresistible urge to travel on but with incredible self discipline and the confirmation there were no chains we overcame over-the-hill-itis and started down. I guess I'm thankful for that, but hope to get back up there again soon.

So after spending most of the day on back roads, in and out of the rain, passing incredible vistas and feeling the fall mountain air of a new winter as it approached, we were given yet another reason to be thankful.

One of the adults carried in some protein for the young.

Shooting a Canon, or a Cannon?

"You shoot Canon don't you?"

"Ya, I've had at least one Canon camera since the early 80s."

"Want to try my 500 mm f 4/L?"

If you are a photographer, you no doubt are saying "WOW." If you aren't you are probably saying "…wonder what's on the next page?"

The day before that conversation, I had received an email from a family friend, one the most successful wildlife photographers I know. It asked if I wanted to meet him at o-dark-

93

thirty the next morning to photograph a flicker nest not far from my place. I jumped at the chance.

Therefore, about 5 a.m. the next morning, we were driving toward the nest, while, at the same time, watching to see what else the morning light was going to show us. We stopped at a blue bird nest but it looked like the babies had already fledged. Driving on, slowly, we saw a doe with a very young fawn nursing, but knew if we stopped, they would be gone before we opened the windows.

Just as the sunlight was getting perfect we arrived at the tree and he asked me if I wanted to use his big lens.

I asked what he had to use and he said an 800mm. So, we really did pull out the "big cannons." We mounted both lenses on tripods and I attached my camera.

It really looked good on that lens, I mean REALLY looked good.

Carrying the equipment to our site I casually asked, "So what does one of these cost new?"

"About $7,000."

"Ha ha, you know, it almost sounded like you said $7,000, ha ha."

"Yes I did."

I had just tossed SEVEN THOUSAND DOLLARS onto my shoulder and was walking through a groundhog city. My ankles were twisting sideways with each step and stumbling seemed eminent, and I had SEVEN GRAND bouncing on my clavicle.

The tired old Toyota I drove wasn't worth that.

At the top of the knoll, as we sat our respective tripods in the tall grass, I realized I hadn't been breathing. Huge inhale!

I looked at his lens and he apparently read my mind.

"About $10,000 new" he said like a businessman talking normal business expenses.

It's a good thing we were outside because I needed a lot of air for a couple minutes.

It didn't take long to be all set up and focused on the hole in the snag. It was about eye level and there was the small head of a young male flicker looking out. I squeezed off a couple exposures and looked at the screen on my camera. Wow!

I stepped back to look at the gear we had just positioned on the knoll. It reminded of the foredeck of the Battleship Missouri I had visited last winter. These were a couple of *big* Cannons.

About now the photographers reading this want to see an image of what those big boys could do. I have included one. The others, if there still are any, want to see a picture of the lenses—I don't have one.

There was a cool breeze but the sky was clear and the morning light just right. We were in a nearly open field dotted by a few trees. Due to the wet, cool spring, the field grass around our legs was just starting to head out. In the distant hills ranged from 4,500 to 6,000. Many of them still had snow. That is unusual for mid June.

I have noticed that we humans who designed seasons based on a man-made calendar are quite flummoxed by the weather this year. I keep reminding myself that nature doesn't always follow our calendar. However, it appears we are starting to get temperatures we consider more normal.

In that clear early morning air, several blue birds and swallows made intricate aerial maneuvers getting insects for babies. Sparrows and finches were winging between the trees finding bits of vegetation for their young. A red-tail Hawk made some "lazy circles in the sky" above us, just like in the Broadway song. The groundhogs, whose city we had traversed, popped up and squeaked at our close proximity to their homes. It was an idyllic spring sunrise.

We were not in a blind, and being quiet wasn't necessary for this kind of shooting so we got to visit as we waited for the parents to bring breakfast. We had some catching up to do as we watched and waited. Regular interruptions stopped conversation

95

when one of the adults carried in some protein for the young. The snapping of shutters was the only noise heard as we worked toward the perfect image. Then back to how life had been happening for us.

We were a couple of 60-somethings just talking. Not trying to impress, or complain, just sharing observations about how we were dealing with adventures given us, some planned and some not.

We joked about how more money was setting on the two tripods than the cost of either of our first homes. We also talked about the pleasure of simply waiting for that perfect picture. And, how glad we are we didn't have to get that perfect picture in order to make the next mortgage payment.

Finally, about eight, the sunlight was getting too flat and it was time to pack up. I took another look at how really cool my camera looked on that big Canon, then removed it and put my 70-300 back on. It still looks pretty cool, and I don't worry so much as I carry it.

By the way, if I'm on your Christmas list... .

She seems to enjoy the bumping and bouncing as we hike the woods.
(Photo © by Ana Huston)

Keeping Wonder Alive, Nature Through a Baby's Eyes

I looked to see who was calling as the phone played its tune; it was my stepdaughter, Ana. Answering, I heard, "gaa ma lalala ba ga."

"Hi Alice," I said. Once again I got "gaa lalala ba."

I thought either nine-month-old Alice is playing with Ana's phone or Ana is having a very bad morning.

Soon Ana came on and said "Hello."

She was just fine and said she had only turned her back for

a second.

I must admit I was enjoying my conversation with Alice, even though I was wondering what she was saying. I'm sure it was, "Let's go for a hike right now!"

Ana and Alice are staying a few miles from here while the Navy sends Noah to school. Something to do with nuclear reactors. He patiently tries to explain it to me but what he tells me sinks in like water on granite. I must admit I love having Ana and Alice here while at the same time seeing the family separated pains me. Once again, those polarities of life which I cannot control surface.

The baby and I had gone for a hike that morning, while her mother took care of a few things around the house. There have been several similar hikes since they came. Mostly we stay on old logging roads, which are more accommodating for her stroller. However, since it does have bicycle tires, it rolls over the rough pretty well. So occasionally, Alice and I take the stroller and do a little "off-roading."

She seems to enjoy the bumping and bouncing as we hike the woods. She is always conscious of the subtleties of life and lives around her. She hears and reacts to even the smallest bird-songs and follows them when they fly. Whenever she hears animal voices, she immediately focuses on their source.

Tall grass brushes her cheeks as we roll by, giving her a new experience and a new discovery, and she uses all her senses to capture each one. With a new texture she will first look, then try to feel, and then, of course, try to smell and taste. She tries out her own voice as the wheels bounce over rocks and sticks, hearing how it changes from rough ground to smooth. It sounds like she enjoys singing while bouncing over rough ground more than on smooth.

Watching her wonder stimulates my own wonder as we trek past dry streambeds, tamarack turning gold and rock faces that rise along our route.

I think of myself as a rather curious person and I enjoy my curiosity but looking at Alice I see absolute wonder in everything.

I am reminded to open all my senses to the world around me, to try, as she does, to explore everything with nothing but wonder. When I reach that goal, the world gets even more exciting.

I have been in all kinds of nature with people who have years of experience and knowledge of their surroundings, people who serve as guides, or teachers of nature. Some are professional; others simply want to be out and are willing to share what they know. In each one, I see a similar curiosity as in Alice: they are conscious of all their life; acutely aware of what surrounds them and their presence in it. They see and make mental notes of every sound, movement, or smell just as Alice does—often with the same wonder, even though years of experience may mean it comes with greater understanding. I like being with these people; it seems all of life is exhilarating for them.

However, what is so fun with Alice is that this is her very first autumn. It isn't that I am showing someone autumn in Idaho for the first time, I love that too. Instead, I have been given the honor to be part of Alice's very first fall. Adding to that I get to show her the North Idaho mountains I love so much.

The curiosity she has now will help open her to the possibilities of the world. Some feel she is too young to understand, but I believe this fall will be as important as all the rest in her life. This fall, and what she learns, will influence how she sees the world wherever that is. In the process, she will learn some things hurt, others do not taste good and she will learn some are fun and do taste good. For me, sharing this fall with Alice will be just as important and influence the rest of my life.

I'm sure there will be more time spent learning to touch something new or in a new way and I'm hoping there will be more phone calls while her mom has her back turned, calls that will keep the wonder in my world alive.

Next to a big Douglas fir and lying in a tight little bundle, was a fawn.

The Baby Trail

I was walking through our woods on the Baby Trail, soaking up a new spring day. The snow had lingered late into the spring and had made it nearly imposable to walk without snowshoes until a couple of days before. As I meandered, I thought of why we had named this trail the "Baby Trail" several years before.

It had been a very similar day and I was in need of some woods time to experience the new spring, so I left my work inside and started a wander. Rounding a bend in the trail I heard some small sounds and looked down. It appeared the ground was moving all around me. I didn't feel anything but there was a lot going on where I stood. I soon recognized that grouse chicks were scurrying in every direction—must have been a dozen or more. Then, to my left, the mama started making noise. First she ran directly at me. I thought it comical that a two-pound bird would try to chase me off but, to her credit, she tried. I stood there watching her and the babies.

When her threat didn't work she suddenly had a broken wing. She started to run away from me with a very convincing "wounded wing" gate. I didn't fall for her "easy prey" scheme, but moved away from the chicks just the same. Not wanting to stress them anymore, or myself over unfinished work, I headed back to the house where my desk waited.

Grouse medicine can be the representation of the sacred spiral. As we travel our sacred journey we circle around to earlier lessons and often get new understandings or completion of old issues. While traveling along our journeys we are ever moving upward, yet always spiraling around past where we have been. It gave me something to think about.

That evening I was telling Linda about the sighting. She wondered if the chicks would still be in the area.

For us, any excuse to take a walk in the woods will do. Even when that excuse is the very unlikely chance that a mother grouse would take her chicks back to the very same place something as big and scary as me had been lurking.

I thought about grabbing a camera but knew we wouldn't see any little birds so left the case closed.

We wandered with Nikki, our dog, slowly in the direction I had gone earlier. Not being real confident in seeing wildlife we were getting caught up with a conversation of the day's activities. Nikki sniffed and smelled her way just ahead of us.

We rounded the bend in the trail and I said, "This is the spot and the babies were mostly running that way." I then turned a bit and pointed in the direction the mama had tried to take me.

As expected, there was nothing there at all. I looked in the opposite direction on the off chance we would see anything. A step and a half from me, next to a big Douglas fir and lying in a tight little bundle, was a whitetail fawn.

The nose of the deer was tight against its left hip, next to its tail. Nikki, standing next to me, hadn't seemed to notice.

I stopped saying whatever I was saying and just pointed; Linda took in a surprised breath. Nikki saw the object of our attention and stretched her nose until one of us called her. Nikki had not moved, but she stepped back looking a bit confused. I was surprised she did not seem to smell it.

Linda half whispered, "Do you have a camera?"

"No."

"It will only take a minute, if you go the short way; see if you can get it."

I left them there and headed through the woods—the most direct route. As quickly as I could and a bit out of breath I was back with a camera and lens. The fawn had not moved. Linda said it had been all she could do not to touch it but she just stayed back and watched for the mother.

We know a doe will clean her offspring by licking around the muzzle and the anus so there is no smell. She will then leave for long periods to forage, since a baby that young could not keep up.

I had no idea how little odor the baby had but Nikki had to see it rather than sniff it out.

Linda also knew mom could be back at any time and might not take her presence lightly, especially since she had a dog with her, so she kept a vigilant eye.

I got on a knee and carefully moved a twig that crossed the babe's face and started snapping. It still did not move. That newborn gave me one of the finest photo ops I have ever experienced.

After a couple dozen shots or so we all left. That infant had not moved for the fifteen minutes as we stood over it.

Deer represents gentleness for some cultures. Looking at that baby there in a bed of pine needles certainly did give us that feeling—gentleness in its infancy.

Even after all these years, as I walk that trail I always think of that spring experience six or seven years ago. My sacred spiral journey continues and with that memory, gentleness fills me.

We have deer in our yard regularly and some, we are quite sure, we have watched mature. We have witnessed the babies and seen their spiral into gentle maturity.

Last November, several does and yearlings were hanging out in our yard. It was the rutting season and they were being wary. Suddenly, a handsome, six-point buck ran out of the trees with amorous eyes. All the ladies and children scattered. He wasn't around long enough to get a photo even if I had been ready. I did get a good look.

It may be hopeful thinking, but I think he was that baby we saw many years ago. Maybe not, but I want to think that.

…another one flew into my view only a few feet from me…

Open and Receptive to all Goodness and Grace

I try to start each day affirming I am open and receptive to all goodness and grace, a practice that allows room for wonderful surprises.

Several weeks ago my inbox contained a note from my friend and fellow wildlife enthusiast, Gary, saying the Snowy owls were in the Polson area and was I interested? My intention of being open to good immediately buried any resistance I may have conjured up. I wrote right back, "I'm all in," without any thought, an opening to a wonderful surprise.

He had contacted a couple other friends who share our curiosity. Sandy is a fellow writer, Brian is a naturalist and adventurer.

That is how I found myself, early one morning, driving into the Flathead Lake region with three friends. The car filled with anticipation, inquisitiveness and keen interest as we drove through the remains of ancient glacial floods in search of the Snowy.

In many cultures, mystery, fear, and wisdom are associated with owls. The Greek goddess Athena carried one on her shoulder symbolizing wisdom. Since most owls are nocturnal, fear of darkness and the unknown surrounds them in mystery. Plus, there is their silence, an absolute silence, when swooping down on unsuspecting prey. Add to that large, round, all-knowing eyes with their uncanny appearance of tracking a full circle, thus giving the feeling of "other worldly" wisdom even in the dark.

The Snowy adds to that mystique their ethereal white color and the fact they are as comfortable hunting in the day as they are at night. For me, light plus wisdom, mystery and silence, gives birth to wonder.

The first one I saw was sitting on a large rock outcrop. The curiosity I had been steeping in for the several hour ride gave way to wonder, excitement, and an indisputable thrill.

Bigger than I expected, though I knew their size, and with a light grey ceiling for a backdrop, ghostly is the only way for me to describe the spirit-like, white presence. Later, while standing, camera ready, another one flew into my view only a few feet from me. I was amazed at the complete silence—even with wings spread to nearly five feet.

To find them on the edge of a town, sometimes sitting on roofs and chimneys, people all around packing SLRs, point-and-shoots and camera phones, created cognitive dissonance with the habitat I know is theirs by nature—the vast, uninhabited wilds of the Arctic.

All was a confirmation: I am supposed to be open and receptive to all the goodness and grace the Universe has planned for me, and it is greater than I could possibly imagine.

I know it is important to remember it as a toy

Toy, Heirloom, and Fireflies

I have lived most of my years in the Northwest, a wonderful place to spend a life, but tonight I saw my first fireflies. While sitting on Ana and Noah's deck in Virginia Beach, Virginia, the little sparkles appeared in the brush beside a nearby pond.

This epic in my life began nearly two years ago in April. Ana was pregnant and for some reason I still don't fully understand, I wanted to build the baby and possible future siblings a rocking boat. After a search on the Internet, a plan that looked good but challenging for my skill level was found.

I ordered the plans, knowing it would be a stretch for my

woodworking abilities; still it needed to be done. Linda does keep reminding me to stretch my body, my mind, and my skills.

It took a while to get started due to some logistics. The kids and soon-to-arrive Alice were in Hawaii at the time, so shipping would be prohibitive. Then orders came for them to move to Virginia Beach. A new question arose: how to get the boat there if it did get built? Finally, last winter, I decided if I didn't build it and get it to them soon Alice would be too old for it. That forced the decision to build and drive it there myself.

Many fears appear whenever I know I'm going to need some skills I have not yet used or developed. For more motivation I told Ana and Noah I was driving back with a surprise for the family, thus removing any safety net and forcing me to dive in and build my first boat.

A friend of mine has told me many times to visualize what I want. So I kept tucked in the back of my mind an image of granddaughter Alice crawling around in the boat.

As work progressed, friends stopped by the shop and talked about the heirloom I was building. In order for a rocking boat to work it must first be used as a toy. It needs to be one that will get scratched and dinged, marred and marked, all in the name of fun and imagination. I could see her looks of determination and her happy grins. I could hear her sweet, petite strong-minded grunts as she crawled around the pint-sized ship and her excited shrieks of joy as she reached each goal. I thought of it as a little vessel of joy for Alice, her friends and future siblings. I knew it was important to remember it as a toy. It may be an heirloom too, but first it must always be a toy.

I varied from the plans slightly to make it look more like an old sailing ship. As I worked, her grandma Linda found a pink flag reading "Pirate Princess;" it seemed to fit so it became a rocking pirate ship.

Another good friend studied the plans carefully and the offered some yew wood for the quarter knees and breast hook.

Yew was commonly used on real sailing ships for those same pieces. All the encouragement and help added depth of community to the venture.

With each construction frustration, I kept that vision of Capt. Alice and her boat in my mind—the project got finished.

Then I started the next phase of the epic. I loaded the little vessel of joy into the back of our truck and drove from North Idaho to the Atlantic Ocean.

The trip was basically as uneventful as a cross-country drive can be. I had some arguments with the GPS, some of which it won, and some I won. I discovered the beauty of the green hills of Kentucky and the deep, tree-covered valleys of West Virginia. The drive was without itinerary. I drove when I felt awake and alert and slept in the back of the truck next to the boat when I needed sleep. Still, somehow between Friday morning and Monday morning I made it to their town. Finally the GPS said, "Turn left" and when I did it said, "Arrive, Ana on right."

Linda flew in that evening and on Tuesday morning Ana and Noah were sent to the store while we kept Alice. While they were gone the ship came into the house and a cute pirate dress, another donation from a good friend, was put on this special granddaughter.

We sat the Captain in her ship when we knew Mom and Dad were in the drive. I felt like the director of a grand production on opening night, waiting to see the reaction of the audience. By the time they came in it had been Alice-tested and Alice-approved.

They were thrilled at the sight, grabbed cameras and camera phones to record the moment. In minutes, Alice and her ship were seen across the nation and around the world by friends and relatives. Later, Noah said he had never received so many comments on one of his Facebook posts.

It isn't woodworking perfection but it is better than I had expected it to be. Alice doesn't seem to mind imperfection as she rocks, crawls and sails through the uncharted territories of her imagination. She is teaching me a little imperfection is perfectly fine.

Building the boat for this family was never about artistic creation but about sharing a dream of mine and giving of myself as an expression of the love I feel for them and from them. It is an honor to be a part of this family.

Finally I fully understand the reason I needed to build the boat.

Tonight the kids went to a movie, not a spontaneous event anymore for them. Linda and I put Alice down and with baby monitor in hand went out on the deck with a glass of wine. That is how I saw my first fireflies.

Just before Alice went to bed she walked over to me, arms raised, wanting to be picked up. I did and started singing to her. She relaxed into me, an arm around my neck, her head resting on my shoulder and became quiet.

That will be my fondest memory of the trip, even more then Alice and the rocking boat.

…and for hikes closer to home in the Cabinets.

The Life of a Knee

Her knee hurts; not constantly, but often enough she has to consider it as she plans activities. Even with planning there are still times she has to stop what she's doing to ice it, and she is sometimes not able to start again.

The surgeon reported that a worn out knee needs to replaced completely, so my wife has a date with an orthopedist in early January.

In January, that time of new beginnings just after the Winter Solstice and the holiday many people call the beginning of a religion, she will have a beginning with her new knee.

The knee that hurts is not a bad joint; in fact, it has served Linda very well. It played softball on the neighborhood diamonds of Cleveland, Ohio many years ago with friends and siblings. There were days of walks and swims at the beaches of Lake Erie and shopping, downtown, on Euclid Avenue or going to the top of the Terminal Tower.

It danced at hops and proms and, as a young lady knee, it walked the halls of hospitals caring for others—some who were having knee surgery themselves. That knee walked campuses at Kent State and later at Metropolitan State in Colorado until she let it carry her to a profession as a nurse practitioner over 30 years ago.

Trekking through the Rocky Mountains of Colorado it explored vistas and waterfalls, ridges and valleys, developing a love for the mountains. That love was rivaled only by a love of walking on ocean beaches, letting the surf roll in around her, sometimes as high as the knee.

This wonderful knee supported pregnancy and parenting as it carried the additional weight and walked the floors rocking and soothing a crying child. Playing, crawling on the floor, helping Ana and her classmates build theater sets in high school and dancing at Ana's wedding were some of the many adventures of motherhood.

Linda knew to take care of herself as she has taught others to do the same, so there were many hours spent in maintenance, doing yoga for flexibility and strength, as well as massages. Maybe this is how she was able to get by longer than many professionals thought would be possible.

She knew that "taking care of it" with rest only would not allow her to live her life fully, so she probably pushed its limits a bit. And perhaps, it also helped keep her leg strong.

That is why as the knee wore it still worked in exam rooms caring for others. It still hiked in the Canadian Rockies climbing steep trails that traversed below glaciers until the winding path reached the top and crossed the ice fields. The knee walked along lakes beneath a canopy of sub-alpine fir and stood for hours watching moose, elk and bears as they browsed. Fields of wild flowers were irresistible as she put light, gentle tracks among them.

One summer she made sure that knee got wet in the Atlantic Ocean at the mouth of the Chesapeake Bay, and later by wading in the Pacific Ocean.

The following winter it walked in the steps of St. Francis and St. Clare on the steep, winding cobblestone streets of Assisi, Italy. Standing in a crowd of thousands the knee celebrated the beginning of a new year on the San Marco Piazza in Venice, discovering new friends in spite of the language barrier.

With her knee she helped the thinning of our forest and brought in several cords of firewood. But the care for the knee wasn't always strenuous. It also experienced the love of a good book, or enjoying fellowship with friends on our deck watching the flickers and nuthatches vie for space at our feeders, and patiently waiting until she could watch the wild animals getting drinks in the back yard. Holidays have been spent relaxing with family and friends sharing meals, sharing gifts and love. Plus there was the support of sitting, often cross-legged, in meditation and contemplation.

Now that the decision has been made, it is time to get even more strength into those muscles around the knee to help the healing process. Exercises directed by a physical therapist are magnetically held to the refrigerator door, and each morning Linda leans against the kitchen island lifting, bending and swinging her legs. While she looks forward to the new knee, she expresses her gratitude for how her body and the "old knee" have supported her thus far in her journey.

This may get us in trouble with some neighbors, but we would like a good snowfall for snowshoeing before she goes in for surgery; her physical therapist said it isn't likely she will get any in afterwards unless spring doesn't come until May or June.

Around the house we are preparing a bedroom downstairs since she can't stress the new knee on the stairs for a few weeks. Folks send emails every day asking if they can get us some meals to have in the freezer. There seems to be some concern about my cooking and Linda's healing at the same time—we have pretty bright friends.

Mostly we are looking forward to the spring. With brisk steps, due to the new knee, she will be out hiking trails looking for wildflowers and trying to spot babies in their natural habitat.

There are plans for strolling beaches in Hawaii as well, climbing to the rim of volcanoes, and for hikes closer to home in the Cabinets, Selkirks and Coeur d' Alenes.

We hope for future trips to the Utah wilderness areas, even to Peru and maybe a trek in Tibet.

Moreover, we will enjoy her new mobility right here taking care of our forest, swimming in the local lakes, picking huckleberries, and dancing—to the music of many talented musicians we know.

My hope is that I can keep up with her.

Views out of the valley are stunning. Henderson Peak, a sharp saw tooth, rises to over 13,500 feet.

Naming Traditions
A New Location on the Map

We finally found all of our gear on a rock beside Alice Lindy Lake. It had been a tiring, eleven-mile day with a net elevation gain of about 1,100 feet. Not bad, but the trailhead was at 9,500 feet.

Alice Lindy Lake is a pure little tarn above the tree line in the Wind River Range of Wyoming. She lies in a basin to the west-southwest of Mount Lester and just south of a long ridge strewn with granite fragments broken from its sheer sides. The Highline trail passes her shore to the north, just before starting a 1,000-foot climb to Lester Pass.

Coming to the lake basin from the northwest, the trail scrambles up a steep and rocky slope before tipping over a lip into a small hanging valley. Views out of the valley are stunning. Henderson Peak, a sharp saw tooth, rises to over 13,500 feet and is only about five-and-a-half miles away. The pinnacle and the glacially marred crest to its south create a horizon to the northwest rivaling any wilderness setting I have ever experienced.

You may wonder why you have never heard of such a wonderful spot. Isolation is not the only reason; the name is not on any maps. I must assume that is simply a gross oversight on the part of cartographers everywhere.

I shouldn't be too hard on them as there is another reason you haven't heard of Alice Lindy Lake.

Alice Lindy is my two-year-old granddaughter. She has never been in the Wind River Range but was in the same state for a few hours a year earlier and she flew over it once.

As we prepared for a hike into the Winds we noticed there were several small lakes that had no names. As I studied the area on Google Earth I saw the same phenomena. So when we needed to tell the outfitter where to leave our stuff, all we could do was point to one of those nameless lochs on the map and say "here," hoping he found the one we intended.

Without geographic names, locating is very difficult. There is the system of longitude and latitude but who can remember all those degrees and minutes and seconds, sometimes even tens and hundreds of seconds?

So I decided to do the world of geography a favor and name this one beautiful little spot after Alice Lindy. After all she is one beautiful little girl, so it seemed to fit.

Alice Lindy Lake is a 5- or 6-acre mere filled with clear pristine water fed by a stream flowing from the side of Mount Lester. The mountain is a rubble-sided, ridge-like peak which dominates views to the east. Its vertical sides rise directly from the basin three thousand feet to its summit. Like all of the range where this pure water lies, the shore is mostly grayish-brown stones, varying in size from baseballs to large trucks; however, the bottom is mostly mud. When we filtered our water we had to be careful not to stir up the dirt and clog the system. Sitting on one of the large boulders just below the water line was the only way to bathe. The water is cold in early September, when we were there. However, it's quite refreshing after a day of hiking or for a morning face wash.

I am not sure what the official system is for naming locations; however, I do know that when a place gets called something long enough by enough people the name sticks, even when it isn't official.

So here is what I did. I took some photos of Alice Lindy Lake and posted them on Google Earth with that name. If this works I'll be looking for a place to name Ernie.

My plan now is to hike back in with Alice someday and show it to her.

One of the guys I was with has a newborn granddaughter. He also found a lake to name. When I told him of my plans to come back with Alice he said, "I don't know, I'll over 80 by then."

I said, "We hear of folks over 80 hiking like this all the time."

"Yeah, but I'm not sure I'll want to."

"If your precious little girl, (and she will always be your precious little girl) wants you to, you will want to," I said.

He laughed and nodded.

We day hiked for the next four days, one of those into Titcomb Basin, a glorious granite cirque gouged out by glaciers. A few remnants still hang on the jagged peaks.

There was a day when we followed Fremont Creek. That day we took a dip in the pool below The Big Waterslide, a natural spillway draining one of those unnamed lakes. The water pours down a stone face about 40 feet high. Never quite free falling but cascading over polished stone, like a slide – thus the name.

It is close to The Jane Lakes, a designation that encouraged me to name Alice Lindy Lake.

117

On each trek back to our base we had to make that steep climb up that very rocky trail into the basin below Lester Peak. Since it always came at the end of the day I started calling it Humor Hill, because I seemed to leave my sense of humor on it each time. I think, considering my attitude, it was a very benevolent name. Others, far less kind, had crossed my mind.

We spent several days exploring the hills and ridges surrounding Alice Lindy. It allowed vistas into many of the valleys and gorges, through passes and gaps of the Winds. Alice is not the only reason I want to go back, the scenery is extraordinary.

After using the wonderful spot I had named as our base for five nights, it was time to start the two-day hike out. We had not arranged for the outfitter so, for the first time on the trip, we carried full packs. The eleven miles were broken up this time by a night on Barbara Lake. I don't have any idea who Barbara is but I bet it was named the same way as Alice Lindy Lake.

The next day we hiked back to the car. By mid afternoon we were sitting in a hot springs and that night rented a cabin where we slept in beds for the first time in two weeks.

In a dream I was hiking with a bright and witty little girl up the hill to Alice Lindy Lake. She named it Ernie Hill.

Hawk appeared in a tree

Claiming My Connection to Spirit The Real Healing Process

A Spirit flew between the sun and me this morning as I sat cross-legged in our woods. The shadow crossed over from south to north, and then circled me completely before pointing toward the source of the midmorning light - the direction of illumination. Through the conifers, I saw the silhouette of Red-tailed Hawk sailing east toward the light.

As a boy, I wondered why I had the name of a bird. In the

119

fifth grade an American Indian was a classmate. He was a friend and could hit a baseball harder than any of the rest of us. One day during lunch, he asked me if Hawk was my totem.

"What's a totem?"

I knew there was a totem pole in the park, but beyond that, I didn't have a clue. He told me a totem was an animal spirit that gave special medicine to help me throughout my life.

That was heathen talk and I knew I wasn't supposed to engage in it at all; in fact, just listening to it could condemn me to eternal damnation.

That evening I asked Dad why our name was a bird. He said the name goes back centuries to England before the Hawks came to the colonies in the early sixteen hundreds, and I was told to be proud of it; I wasn't so sure.

A few days later, I got in a fistfight with my friend. For years I didn't know why we had fought.

That was my first fight with the Great Spirit; a fight with my fears, the first of many. That fight with Spirit dominated most of my life. I didn't throw a fist again, but I hurt.

While attending a Christian boarding school, my body didn't recover from strenuous activity like the other guys; in football I didn't heal like my teammates, and in track I thought I just couldn't get in shape, because I was always sore and stiff. During college, my muscles would not stretch, and I never felt limber. At the same time, I was holding firm to my rigid concept of God, trying to avoid any thought of a bigger spirit.

Hiking for days in the woods, I always felt at one with nature. It was obvious to me that the forest as a whole - trees, brush, streams, even the land - was an expression of God. Yet I could not bend the rule that God was somewhere far away in Heaven.

How could a God create all I saw but not be there? How could I be created in the image and likeness of God and not have God within me?

These questions made me feel alone. Entertaining them was not okay. Still, even after losing track of my friend from grade school, the memory of totems and animal medicines had planted the seed of a holistic God, though I would not nurture it.

In my circle of friends, books about Native American life and history were popular, rather trendy even. *Black Elk Speaks, Seven Arrows* and several others were making the rounds. As I read them, a God consistent with my feelings emerged. Others read the books and learned of a culture both ancient and present. I discovered The Great Spirit. Still, my fear kept me from allowing any flexibility in the Christian God I thought I knew.

All the while, my body was getting rigid and bent, my shoulders stooping forward as if closing around my heart. Walking and hiking became difficult so I started riding my bicycle as a way to get out.

I had seen several physicians; all of them said I had some kind of arthritis and after several years one diagnosed *Rheumatoid Spondylitis*. By then I was in my early thirties and the Doc said I would continue to lose ambulation, and probably be wheelchair bound by my mid forties.

I could not accept that. I started spending even more time on the bike, sometimes 200 miles a day, not realizing Spirit was putting me there. The constant aerobic work was slowing the disease but not curing it.

Completely falling away from the traditional church, I immersed my spare time in nature, all the while self-medicating the pain- physical and emotional- with drugs and alcohol.

During one of those bicycle tours, I found myself resting on a log on the Washington Coast, exhausted after several miles on the bicycle and feeling hopeless. The sky was gray; one of those famous northwest drizzles was soaking into everything. My joints felt resistant to any movement and my emotions were as soggy as the day. Normally, I don't mind misty wet days, having clothes and gear to be in it, but that day I was not happy.

Looking around at the trees, so damp, the colors so saturated in the moisture, I wished I had something for the pains, all of them. The thought of an hour or so ride to a liquor store for some medication surfaced, except the hurting prevented movement. I wondered if this was going to be my last bike tour- if I would even finish this one.

To have rain flow over me often feels cleansing after a day on the bike but that day it wasn't happening. What I felt instead was frustration and anger flowing over me. My body was failing me.

There was a stream next to the log where I sat. It splashed down the hill behind me, bubbling over some rocks before flowing onto the sand, creating tiny temporary streambeds as it made its way to the surf. It gave me little comfort as I sat absorbed in my feelings.

Overhead I heard wings forcing air. Hawk appeared in a tree that bent over the rock-strewn brook. By then I knew about Hawk and that its medicine was the Messenger of the Spirits. Watching it, mostly out of curiosity, the memory of my childhood friend came back. Looking up with rain, and some tears, washing my face I asked the majestic bird, "Are you my totem or is my name simply a centuries-old coincidence from another land?"

The bird did nothing, but in only a few moments I felt lighter, much like after medicating, though I hadn't drank or smoked anything.

We just sat looking at each other, bathed by the precipitation, and listening to the creek, the ocean waves, to the dripping of moisture off the leaves, the wild flowers and the trees on the hills behind us.

Thinking about that question, the realization came that I had never asked it before.

With that thought in my consciousness, the bird opened his big round wings and lifted. He lifted, didn't start a dive to pick up air speed, just lifted. The fog was not moving and the rain fell straight down. I didn't feel any breeze that could raise a bird like that; it had the appearance of an ascension. Tipping slightly, he disappeared over the hill to the east.

I tried to make some sense of what had happened, but that quickly gave way to wonder because, upon standing, my body felt healthier.

Scrambling up the hill and looking out at the fog-shrouded ocean, then east to the misty hills where Hawk had gone, my body had a new energetic feel. The climb took some effort but was fun. I wasn't free of pain but a lightness filled me, physically and emotionally. And my joints and muscles felt like they belonged to someone MY age - or younger.

What was going on? This didn't fit into my thinking; I had seen hawks thousands of times in my life, so it couldn't have anything to do with that bird. He had just wanted something to eat or to drink from the stream and my presence had frightened him.

My body was feeling better and my mind was clear. Nevertheless, things were confusing. Hawks had appeared to me repeatedly- even in my name.

Reflecting on what had happened the only difference was my question, the fact *I* had taken an action. Did that mean I had claimed my connection to Spirit?

This whole medicine and Hawk thing was getting a little out of hand- a scary superstition.

The most daunting part of that day was I wasn't in any way impaired. I was going to remember this tomorrow and for many more tomorrows to come.

And, there was the question: if I am the messenger, what is the message? How will I know it when I see it?

The next few days I rode home with a new awareness, thinking about the time with Hawk on the coast. Riding across the arid scablands of Eastern Washington the hawks didn't just sit on poles and posts as usual. They appeared to be enchanted by my presence and kept flying between me and the sun, casting their shadows lightly over me.

Could I become the messenger? Or, was I already?

I had been directing plays for years. Some were thought-provoking, others comedies. It was good work, giving the audiences some insights or entertainment. Wasn't that delivering a message?

The pain and stiffness started to subside as if a conflict had been taken from my body. Occasionally, others noticed I was standing straighter.

I heard the local Unity Church was doing a series on the mythologist Joseph Campbell, one of my heroes, and I decided to attend, but had no intention of getting involved with a church.

There, for the first time, I was introduced to a metaphysical approach to the Bible and its teachers, an approach which melded with the concept of a holistic God that I had stuffed for so many years.

It affirmed I am part of creation, and thus one with God. Even more, I was responsible for owning that oneness, and owning my healing. The pain was a part of me that needed to be recognized before it could be released. I needed to thank it for bringing me to this place before I could let it go. If I did not recognize it I would have nothing to release, it would be another way of holding on through denial.

Once that understanding was in place there was one more step. I could not take ownership of anything that was not God-like in me - the rheumatism. I needed to recognize I was holding onto thoughts that were not allowing me to be whole. It was my responsibility to thank them and let them go. I was not a victim of circumstance.

It required a new attitude, one that only let me own perfect health rather than illness, one that focused on the sensation of more flexibility every day in my body, not on pain and stiffness.

Still, the conflict didn't disappear altogether but manifested in more questions. Who had I come here to be? Writing became my source of delivery; it was more personal- my story.

One morning while meditating on the bank of a creek flowing from the snows of Mt. Hood, I received a bigger meaning of being The Messenger. I am not a courier, not one who delivers a message and moves on- I must *be* the message.

Today, I know Hawk is my totem and its medicine is the Messenger of the Spirits. That is something I am proud to claim. It is who I came here to be, with a connection to Spirit that is not in conflict with the universal God I wanted to love, not fear.

The questions are still appearing; for example, where do I deliver the message? Could it be the message is not to move through me but is for me? Is that what it means to be the message?

This story first appeared Science of Mind Magazine.

"I am going into this with the intention that it will go as well or better than the last one. I want you to have that intention also."

A Hike That May Change Our Lives

When we came to the fork in the trail it had just started raining. As Linda pulled the hood of her raincoat up she eyed the tracks ahead.

"The one to the left will have us back to the car in ten minutes; the one to the right will be well over an hour." I said. "How are you feeling?"

She said "Fine, let's go this way," and turned right.

We were in a fairly dense conifer forest with a few openings but no expansive views. Even with the nearly closed canopy the rain was getting to the vegetation on the floor along with the rain gear we had on.

It was after dinner before we had headed out for a refreshing and stretching walk. Almost as an afterthought we grabbed jackets and stuffed them in a daypack. Since it was only a couple days after the summer solstice, light still filtered through the trees, even though it was well into evening.

We had been out for about a half hour when we came to the junction in the trails so her decision, which is the one I had hoped she would make, added considerably to the overall walk.

Not much was happening in the woods since the weather kept most animals and birds under protection. They, no doubt, wondered what the emergency must be for us to need to be out.

It really was not an emergency but it was important that we walk. Linda had just had her right knee replaced two weeks before. This wasn't the first walk since then but would prove to be the longest.

It had been three-and-a-half years since she had her left knee replaced, and it changed our lives. For a couple of years she had no pain. It allowed for some very extensive hiking and snowshoeing, including several mountain hikes and camping trips in the Cabinets and the Coeur d' Alenes, as well as the Canadian Rockies. Rivers and streams had been crossed and she was victorious over some challenging elevations. In Hawaii she swam in the ocean and, with a granddaughter on her back, climbed to the top of Diamond Head. She covered the entire historical city of Williamsburg, Virginia while keeping up with that same child.

I think the most important thing it let her do, pain free, was be a grandmother. And soon another grandchild would be taxing her stamina.

For several months the right knee had been giving her the same discomfort the first one had, so it was time to see the surgeon again.

He told her that the first procedure had been quite difficult yet her recovery had been incredible. "That may not happen this time," he said. "There is always a chance for complications."

Linda thanked him and said she knew that, and she knew he had to tell her that.

Then she said, "I am going into this with the intention that it will go as well, or better, than the last one. And I want you to have that intention also."

He said he was "all in" with that attitude and they, once again, formed a partnership in her healing.

So the walks we greeted summer with were slower and shorter than other summers, but each one had been a challenge that had been met with enthusiasm.

The first one was a lap around the hospital room in late afternoon the day of the operation. Each one after progressed until we were back walking in the woods we love so much.

The trail had some steeper slopes, both up and down, than she had done post-op, yet still we trekked on. The only complaint was she did not feel comfortable looking up since there were so many roots in the trail. Finally, a half-mile from the car, our course leveled without as many obstacles to trip over and the pace picked up a bit. The rain did not let up and we marched on, feet getting wet from the grass, but in good spirits.

Back at the car, I started the fan to keep the windows from fogging and we peeled out of wet jackets. It had been a fun, good and challenging hike and Linda, once again, triumphed.

Back home, ice was applied to the knee and ibuprofen helped with some soreness. She has not taken any other painkillers for several days—says she doesn't need them.

It had not been a long hike but, under the circumstances, it was a very successful trek that could very well change our lives.

Breathe in the Healing Breath of Spirit

When I asked anyone who had experienced an inguinal hernia repair how it felt, they always answered with, "Well, it hurt some."

During my first meeting with surgeon, Dr. Thilo, before the surgery he said "when the local wears off you will be a little mad at me." I didn't know what was meant by that since I had never heard local used that way.

Except for tonsils, over 50 years earlier, I've never had a surgery and all I remember from that was getting all the ice cream I wanted. I had no expectations in my mind.

So early one January morning Linda took me into the day surgery at the Medical Center for a quick fix. Linda, my wife, is a nurse practitioner, so she knows how medical stuff works. Add to that she is a very spiritual nurse, so she told me when there is pain to "breathe into it with the healing breath of Spirit." I believe this, too, but was wondering how it applied to surgery.

The RN who came to the waiting room for us, it turned out, was someone I had known several years ago but had lost contact with. I didn't even know she had become a nurse.

We walked back to the pre-operation room talking about old times. I was placed in a big blue recliner inside a curtained cubical and she started an IV painlessly and plumbed it to a bag over my head. Her body piercing of my arm was so painless I wondered if she did tattoos also, but didn't ask.

She and Linda talked "nurse talk" and made sure I knew why each procedure was needed.

After a few minutes, Linda and I were left alone. She reminded me that there would be some pain, and to just "breathe the healing breath of Spirit" into the pain.

Soon a "relaxer" was injected into the intravenous tube in

my arm.

Whoa! That cleared the fuzz off some old (but fond) memories from the late 60s. Linda smiled a knowing smile as the nurse stepped behind the recliner and said it was "kiss time." Linda and I did. Then one of them asked how I was.

"Just lookin' for fun an' feelin' groovy."

Linda left. Soon, the big blue recliner started to move out of the cubicle and taxied across the room toward a couple of big doors. We passed several other curtained cubicles along the way. Most of them had folks wearing the latest hospital fashions, looking rather apprehensive. In my head I heard the song, "Don't you worry 'bout a thing" and hoped they could hear it too.

Things started to cut out at this point, even though they said I would be conscious during the operation.

On the warm table in the operating room lots of green-covered creatures without faces were busy arranging and doing "surgical stuff." They all seemed to know exactly what was needed and worked efficiently.

Another green-covered creature came in who did have a face. I recognized him as Dr. Thomas Thilo, the gifted and trusted surgeon. He is a tall, confident and caring man with a great sense of humor, kind of an Alan Alda type. His only concern seemed to be my well-being, and I knew he would buck the system to make that happen. I was glad he was in charge. Or maybe it was that relaxer. "Just lookin' for fun an' feelin' groovy."

Soon I noticed his face also disappeared. I was enjoying a low degree of consciousness, a little like a '60s Saturday night flashback.

I have some memories of being on the table but I can't fully verify them by putting two together in a row.

I do remember being put back into the big blue recliner and taxied into another room full of curtained cubicles.

Others were already in some of the cubicles looking rather ethereal but coming down.

They brought me some coffee and toast. That was good because I had the munchies bad. I think it was the stuff in the IV tube.

Linda and Dr. Thilo came in looking pleased; I think they had already been talking in medicalese. Doc told me it had gone very well but added, "When the local wears off and you try to move, you're going to be a little mad at me."

I was more interested in finding out when I could get back to important things, like snowshoeing.

There began to be a little discomfort in my gut, so someone left to get some meds. Linda said to "breathe into it with the healing breath of God… and take the meds."

I was wheeled out to the car where Linda was waiting. I didn't remember her leaving before me to get the car.

We made the 25-mile drive to our peaceful home in the woods. It went well, but the fuzziness returned to the memories of the '60s. It's better to leave them that way, quite fuzzy.

Feeling way past due for a nap, I sat in my favorite chair and dozed off. When I woke up, I needed to use the bathroom.

As I got up I was kicked. It was a direct, hard kick in the very low abdomen. It was a pitiless kick committed by a brutally outraged, overly steroided, cosmic mule on crack.

I wanted to scream. Not a grunt or moan like a quarterback makes when he's blindsided by a 300 pound linebacker. No, I wanted to scream, scream like a bobcat when it is in the death throes of a territorial battle. But I couldn't scream. The pain had sucked every milliliter of air out of my body. There wasn't air enough to make a vocal cord rattle, let alone a scream.

Linda said "Breathe into it, breathe in the…." I couldn't breathe anything. I felt like a plastic garbage bag when it's pulled out of the box and you can't figure out which end is supposed to open.

That is when I found out what is meant by local. I also noticed Tom "the Slasher" Thilo was no place to be found so I could affirm his prediction that "I was going to be a little mad at him when it wore off." The highest my torso could get was parallel with the floor.

Linda said she thought she had married a much taller man. Her sister thought it would be a good time to give me the vacuum.

Linda helped me move, but it was only slightly faster than a mature Ponderosa pine with a 10-foot taproot anchored into the earth. I felt about as flexible as a steel beam used as a bridge girder.

Back in my chair, I started breathing and yes, I wanted all of that healing breath now!

Somehow, something got through the haze and I realized, to heal, I needed to thank everyone who had been part of this. Starting with the valet parking attendants through everyone involved and back to the guy who opened the door and helped me back into the car. I also knew I needed to thank Great Spirit, who had handpicked each and every one of these fine and skilled people for their expertise and caring. And, for Linda, as well as all the people who had kept me in their thoughts and prayers.

It's been a while now since the surgery. My mind has cleared as much as it ever will, and I've been at full height for several days.

The thank-yous I gave seemed to have opened up my heart to healing.

Dr. Thilo called to see how I was. When I joked with him about how "I was a little mad at him when the local wore off" he said, "That's why we do outpatient." I can't blame him for that, it's true I was mad but I doubt if I could have done anything with that pain in my gut.

A friend called who said he heard I had just done the hernia thing. He said he needed to do it pretty soon too.

"How does it feel" he asked

"Well," I said thoughtfully, "it hurt some".

This 80-pound pal loved the out of doors even more than I do

Lessons From Glacier

Lately I've been thinking about lessons we learn from the animals in our lives. Glacier, a white German Shepherd, taught me a great deal about unconditional love and how to lighten up and have more fun.

All Glacier ever needed for a toy was a stick, and nearly any stick he could pick up was fine. On several occasions the stick was, in reality, a branch or root that had a Ponderosa attached to one end, but he would give it a valiant effort just the same. When it wouldn't move he simply had more fun finding another one.

I think Glacier wanted to have a pet of his own. He would spend hours trying to draw a squirrel down a tree, just for the fun of it. Another pet that intrigued him were the chipmunks; he was always excited in spring when they started running around. As soon as they ran into their hole he would stick his nose in to see what was going on. Imagine being four inches long and suddenly a snout longer than your body, and with bad breath, appeared in your home. He simply wanted to join them in their fun; they didn't seem to understand.

It is said people and their dogs look alike. Glacier always received compliments on how good-looking he was.

When I needed to talk he was always willing to listen without judgment or advice, just listen. When I did some favor for him he just received it. He didn't say, "I'll do you a favor tomorrow," or "Don't do that for me," or "Now I owe you." He knew he was deserving and simply accepted it.

This 80-pound pal loved the out-of-doors even more than I do and his name was perfect. When the snow fell he couldn't be happier. As soon as he was in fresh snow he started rolling on his back, making a Shepherd's version of snow angels. When the mercury reached about 65 degrees he was looking for shade. But was always willing to go hiking or be with me when working around the place, no matter how high the temperature, even though his comfort level was in the cooler ranges.

One hot day the stresses of life were weighing heavy on me. After observing my inability to cope for quite a while, Glacier started walking away from the house. He took only a few steps when he stopped and looked back, as if to say, "Follow me." At first I didn't understand. He wasn't a Rin Tin Tin or a Lassie, so I wasn't used to him taking me somewhere to rescue someone in distress. In fact, I think that might have been the only time he wanted me to follow him. But he finally got through my self-absorbed whining and convinced me to follow along.

Starting up a hill behind the house and into the woods, I trailed behind. When I stopped to look at the sights he stopped, but kept encouraging me to move on. So I did.

I started wondering if he had found an abandoned mine shaft with an injured child in it and we were going to be heroes, or some other kind of high drama. I started getting into the hike, wondering if this dog should have his own TV show.

As we came out on a rock overlooking the valley, a place where I have sat and contemplated the beauty of my surroundings many times, I stopped and turned around for a quick look. It was perfect. A hawk was gliding over the valley looking for a meal. Close by, the chickadees and wrens were singing and winging in the trees. Across the valley a doe grazed on some leaves between glances at us to see if we were staying a safe distance.

When I turned back to follow Glacier on his epic, he was laying in the shade of a spruce tree taking a nap. That is when I realized he knew what I needed - to get out and relax, maybe meditate, and this was the perfect place to take me. I looked back out over the valley and wondered if Glacier had the birds and the deer on retainer just for a perfect moment like this. Probably he was tired of listening to me grouse about the dire condition I thought I was in, but he knew what to do. So we spent some time there on that rock, Glacier, me and God, fixing me, at least for the moment.

I've been thinking I need to go back to that place again. Last week my pal, Glacier, finished his work on earth and moved on. Naturally I miss him, but more than that I appreciate him for the lessons and gifts he left with me.

Thanks, Glacier, for stopping by and giving me a few years.

Being Mindful

I had pulled a sled full of firewood to the porch and up the three steps for unloading under the roof about a thousand times. On this Sunday afternoon there was a light snow falling with a little breeze as Linda and I chopped. After loading the sled, I headed for the porch. A dusting of fresh powder was blowing under the roof onto the deck as I turned around to wrench the sled up the steps.

I gave a good hard tug and both feet let go of the slick surface and flew. I caught a lot of air and a little hang time before I landed hard on the small of my back, nothing breaking the fall— just me slamming onto the frozen boards.

A loud, involuntary groan whooshed out from my lungs and throat and soared on the cold wind across the yard and into the woods. Linda, still at the woodshed, was alerted by the sound. She looked to see what had happened but couldn't see me, on my back, so shouted "what's up - where are you?"

Lying there in the snow on the porch my first thought was "How many stupid pills did I have to take to pull this off so successfully?"

Linda was running, the best she could while being more mindful of ice and snow than I had been. Her face was a graphic image of concern. I yelled I had not hit my head, then muttered, "I wouldn't be hurting so bad if I had."

When she got to me I was sitting up, in pain, snow melting through my jeans and self directed anger firmly in control of my mental state.

I think one reason Linda is in my life is to tell me when I'm really not being kind to myself—to look at myself through a more compassionate heart, the way she looks at me. So she pointed out, in her always-gentle way, the worst thing I could do now was beat myself up, to claim to be stupid. She pointed out I had made a mistake and now I needed to start the healing process—being angry was only going to postpone or prevent that from happening.

139

In my state of mind I heard "Don't be so stupid as to call yourself stupid just because you did something stupid."

She read my mind and said softly, "You are not stupid."

Even through the murky haze of pain I knew she was right. I needed to get 'stupid' out of my head and start listening to what I needed.

She asked if I could feel my feet; yes, I could. She carefully bent my knees; they worked fine. The back hurt, but there were no shooting pains down my legs. I was sure I wasn't severely injured and no surgery would be necessary even though the pain was nearly unbearable. I had seriously insulted my body.

Linda asked what I thought I needed.

What a brilliant question. What did I need? It forced me to focus on my healing instead of on what had happened.

I heard again, "What do you need?" I felt getting up and beginning to move would help. So that's where we began.

Painfully, as my body was moving into recovery mode, I started to get up with her assistance. Inside the house she helped me out of boots and wet clothes while gently touching around my back and spine asking if there were any additional pains. She is always a nurse practitioner. Still, I was sure I was only hurting— no serious injuries.

Because of her questions I listened to what I felt. Walking around the house for a bit seemed right, and a trekking pole helped. After a couple laps, ice seemed to be needed. I tried both for a while before sitting down with the ice on my back.

A Sunday afternoon alone at home with my wife is precious time to me. I had been enjoying our day jointly doing chores, even working on taxes together, which brought back some fond memories. There had been a snowshoe trek in our woods with Nikki, our dog, playing and making new tracks ahead of us on the trail, while the snow was loading the trees.

After bringing in some wood we were going to grill some steaks and open a favorite bottle of wine.

But now, I could only concentrate on trying to get comfortable.

The anger started to surface again and I began to mutter.

Linda pointed out, ever so gently, that I was not helping the healing process.

Okay, back to what it was I needed.

I was in the middle of "Another Flippin' Learning Opportunity" or as I like to call it, an AFLO.

There had been stresses earlier in the day, which is where my mind had drifted. I was not present with the task. I am smart enough not to pull hard backwards while standing on a slick surface, yet that is exactly what I had done.

So I did it, and there were consequences that needed to be healed. The only way to do that was leave it in the past.

I also needed to forgive myself, not only for making the mistake but also for berating myself for doing it. This is not a new thought to me; in fact, I have helped others through exactly the same process.

It brought me back to forgiveness.

It is my responsibility to manage my thoughts. The stresses didn't cause the accident; I was simply not paying attention.

So I had the opportunity, for several days, to allow someone else to care for me, and to be caring to myself. It was a chance for me to be with me, to remember I am not stupid and I do deserve to be cared for.

Now I'm feeling good again and trying to put the lessons of that Sunday into daily practice.

Memories, Music and Angels

It was a Monday morning; I was drinking coffee and thinking about the work ahead for the day. Linda had just left for her office.

Outside a bright day was dawning. The brush around the house was turning red and yellow. A quick look out the window and I knew a short walk in the woods seemed to be in order before sitting down at my desk.

Being outdoors always seems to be a priority. As I headed down a trail I noticed my phone was still in the house – oh well. The birds were happy with another warm, fall day. A squirrel rushed about taking advantage of the weather, dropping cones from a Douglas fir on the trail. The tamaracks were starting to turn and the pine's inner needles were getting brown.

I could hear the music of the dry fall day. The grass as it broke under my steps, the brittle leaves falling off the brush as I walked by, all of it was accompanied by birds with varied voices and chattering small animals.

There has always been music in my life and sometimes the orchestra is nature.

My mind could not help but follow a trail to work so I reluctantly went back to the house.

While I was out, there had been a call. It was the nurse at the assisted care facility where mom lives. She said mom had fallen in her bathroom and they had called an ambulance.

I headed toward the car with phone in hand this time. I called the hospital. Mom appeared to have a shoulder injury and a some bad looking wounds – one on her elbow, and one on an ankle, as well as a hard hit on her head. I called Linda.

During the 45 minutes getting to town in Monday morning traffic, I tried not to let fear take over, her 89 years added to my concern.

I wanted to bring back the music of the morning in the

forest. When that failed, the music my mother had introduced me to as a child started floating around in the recesses of my mind. Mom said many times all music is from angels.

At the hospital they sent me to a room in the ER. It was empty. I assumed Mom was in X-ray so just hung out. It was easy to absorb the intensity of the place and my anxiety level started to climb like a cat running from a coyote.

A fellow in scrubs wheeled mom into the room; she looked little and frail on the gurney. When she saw me, she grabbed my hand. Tears ran onto her pillow as she told me how much it hurt.

I found myself traveling back in time 50 some years when I had fallen out near the barn and was hurting. Mama, as always, suddenly was there. She was tall, strong, and beautiful. In my mind I could hear music – it seemed to accompany her whenever she comforted me. There were violins and harps, so it must have been her angel friends, and they made the hurt go away.

In the ER I tried to make mom's hurt go away.

"I was so afraid they would never find me," she said as the pain and fear griped her.

Maybe her angel friends would show up just like they used to.

A doctor came in and said he had ordered some pain meds. "They had trouble in X-ray shooting her shoulder because of the discomfort," then he grinned at me and said, "We'll get her really stoned and send her back for more films."

Angels come in all shapes and sizes.

Just as they were taking her away again, Linda came in. She had found coverage for her own patients so she could be here and help me. Being in the profession, she can explain to me what was going on. Linda is definitely one of my angels.

When they brought mom back this time, the pain meds were wearing off. Linda saw me react to the way mom was feeling and told me to "sit over there." I did. She and the doctor talked about the fracture and that they could not operate because of her

144

weak heart. Then Linda looked at me and said, "When they come in to set this bone, you will need to run some errands." It must have been obvious that I couldn't handle my mama's hurting any better than I can handle my own.

When they sent me away I wandered the halls until I found a door saying Meditation Chapel. It felt like a good place to be. Sitting, listening to a fountain that bubbling in the corner, memories of Mom flowed in.

One was years ago in parents home. I was in the basement and Dad's shotgun shell reloading equipment was on the shelf behind a big old steel washtub I could just barely see over. The clothes washer drained into the tub. I climbed up and into the tub, which allowed me to reach a can of gunpowder on the shelf. While I was there the washer started to drain, but I didn't let that stop me. When I turned there was mother, tall and strong. I was about three and a half feet tall, standing knee deep in dirty, soapy laundry water, a can of gunpowder in my hand. Mom walked slowly, deliberately, her hands at her sides. With each step one foot was placed directly in front of the other. She had only one of her angel friends with her. It was whistling the theme from "The Good, The Bad and the Ugly." I never did that again.

That was enough meditation, so I walked out to the street. As the memories of Mom and her angels stayed with me, I wished I could be one for her now.

On the street thoughts transported me once again to childhood. I was in the seventh grade band and had been asked to march in a parade with the eighth and ninth graders. Mom made sure I had the new white shoes to go with the uniform along with the blue wool trousers with a white stripe, a double-breasted royal blue jacket with white lapels and white patent leather belt. A military-style cap with a small bill and a white plume sticking straight up topped it all. When I think back, I kind of looked like an over-dressed quail.

Marching down the street with the music echoing between

145

the buildings, I knew where my family would be. As we approached I let my eyes slide off the lyre holding the music. There they were, Mom tall and strong with tears on her cheeks, waving a little flag and keeping time with the rhythm. Her angels were giving a rousing performance of a Sousa march and I was playing third trombone with them.

Back at the street next to the hospital I wondered if that arm would ever wave a flag again.

A kid, doing what kids do, squealed his tires at the corner. I remembered being 16; Mom and Dad had just bought a brand new '63 Studebaker. A friend and I were putting it through its paces when I lost it and the left rear tagged a post. It broke the light and put a small dent in the fender.

I went home. It was late, Mom came out of her room and asked how I was.

"Fine," I said.

"Good," she said.

I looked away and told her when the car was parked in front of Steve's house, someone hit the back corner.

She said, "Look at me."

By then I could look over head her without stretching, but I still remember her as tall.

She took a breath then told me what had happened, when, where, and what time. She gave me the complete details, all to the accompaniment of an angel combo playing the theme from "Shaft." Boy I was busted, thanks to living in a small town.

Linda found me wandering on the street and we walked back to the ER. Mom was asleep on the bed, a tiny body with its arm in a cast. The bump on her head looked like a purple tennis ball. She was little, old, and broken.

We sat there quietly waiting for her to be transferred to a room. Perhaps just being there and calling for angels was a way I could be an angel for her.

I wondered what her angels were playing for her as she

slept. Maybe Bach, as she was always partial to the baroque. But she liked the romantic too, so maybe it was Tchaikovsky. No, I bet it was something out of her old Lutheran hymnal. Whatever it was, I'm sure the angels were there, comforting and holding her while taking the pain away.

When Will Justice Be Served?

When all people who want to meet in peace and love can do so
without any fear,
Then justice will be served.
When all people realize violence only begets more powerful
violence,
Then justice will be served.
When we all understand the joy of our unity through our diversity
and know that love is much more powerful than any violence,
Then justice will be served.
When I am one with the peace in my heart and have complete
forgiveness even for those who feel they need to destroy me,
Then justice will be served.

Confessions of a Volunteer

In our culture, the non-profit organization fills a valuable role, and most function with a volunteer work force. Which has quite an advantage for the budget; however, without pay or promotion to compensate effort, there is potential for complication. How do you get people to fulfill their commitments? It is true they must have a sense of dedication to the association; on the other hand, they are primarily working for a personal intrinsic reward.

Let me tell you a story. This is, of course, a fictional story and only a figment of my imagination. If this story resembles any meeting you, or someone you know, may have attended it is purely a coincidence - and I'm sorry.

I walked into a meeting for an organization where I volunteer. I wasn't very excited about attending the meeting; still, I felt it was important for the organization so I showed up. I sat down and noticed there were ten chairs set up; four of the chairs were empty.

Right away, I felt righteous indignation welling up in me. After all, those chairs should be full, if I bothered to get here so should they. They should have at least called.

That is when the *should* hit the fan. All six of us jumped right in and started flipping *should* all over those empty chairs and the folks who were not sitting in them. After all, they should know how important this is, and we shouldn't have to kick *should* all over them to get them there. It didn't take long, and the whole place was a pile of *should* and it appeared nobody wanted to join in keeping their commitment. I wonder why?

As I separate from the story, my first thoughts center on reasons behind the frustration and anger.

Fear is the basis for all anger, and frustration is a mild form of anger. If this is true then what are my fears around this issue?

Am I afraid people are not respecting something I think is important? If that is the case, maybe they do not respect me either. Do I fear that something I think is important really is not, and consequently, I am wasting my time? Am I afraid this organization, or project, which has value to me, will fail?

It doesn't take long for that kind of thinking to turn into a downward spiral ripe for destruction with no good possible ending.

It is even more dangerous when several people share these fears and show it with righteous anger. Their perceived problems may not allow them to see, or feel, the negativity being created. In fact, they may feel productive, when really they are not seeing or addressing the true issue. It is very possible they are looking the wrong way.

Nothing is wrong; there has simply been an oversight or an out of sight.

Here is another story of a volunteer meeting. Once again, this is strictly fiction and any resemblance to a meeting you, or someone you know, may have attended is - well, good.

I walked into a meeting for an organization where I volunteer. I wasn't very excited about attending the meeting; still, I felt it was important for the organization so I showed up. I sat down and noticed there were ten chairs set up; six of them were full.

Before the meeting started someone in the group made sure the other five in attendance looked at the sixth and thanked them for showing up. Then, that ritual moved around the group until everyone had thanked everyone, and each one was thanked by each of the others. When they finished the members not in attendance, for whatever the reason, were thankfully remembered for their support of the whole. Wherever they were and whatever they were doing, they were acknowledged and held with care and respect, and then the meeting began.

In the second story, care and respect for everyone filled the place. The members there were recognized and thanked; those who were not there were also recognized. It is a change of focus. There is no doubt in my mind a meeting room filled with respect and gratitude will be more attractive and productive than a room containing a pile of *should*.

While it is true that a commitment appeared to be broken, it is important for all volunteer organizations to create pleasant and inviting environments.

Let me tell you another story. Again if it resembles anything which may have happened to you, it is a coincidence, and I'm sorry.

"Ernie will you join this committee? We desperately need your skills. We meet once a month for a couple of hours."

Boy is my ego pumped. Because, what I hear is, "I am the only one with the skills they need and it's only a couple hours a month, for something I feel is necessary."

I attend the first meeting and find out my skill set is needed on a subcommittee that is working on an important ongoing project.

Do you see what is coming? The commitment has gone from of couple of hours a month to an important ongoing project. Guess who wasn't there, when the first project meeting came on the same date I had another commitment?

Those who did show up started flipping *should* all over me. It didn't feel good. I said I would serve, but only a couple hours a month. I felt the task was not fully represented. Feeling valued got in my way, and I did not bother to get clear on the task. In the end I started feeling resentful.

It is easy to say when someone agrees to a commitment, follow through is expected. However, (and this is a big however), was the expectation made perfectly clear? Did a two-hour-a-month commitment become many more hours out of an already busy life? Remember these are volunteers with busy lives.

When the people feel strongly enough about an organization to consider volunteering, they deserve to have a clear understanding of exactly what they are agreeing to. To assume they will know because they understand "how business works" is a disservice to the people and the organization. When the expectation is clear, before a volunteer commits, they have a better understanding of the job and its value. This creates a much better prospect for a quality member.

Unfortunately, sometimes commitments can't be fulfilled. It is even more unfortunate when people need to be replaced because they can't meet their commitment. When that happens it is better, and far less frustrating, to have an unfilled position than to have only good intention sitting in an empty chair.

Then, at each meeting, make sure everyone is appreciated—even the leaders—and those who are not there are remembered, and honored, so the meeting begins in a positive uplifting light.

Remember each of the stories used here are fictitious. But, if the *should* fits…

Next time try a more rewarding approach, isn't that why we volunteer anyway?

As I walk the joy and companionship of these pets fills my thoughts with thankfulness for them. (Photo © by Linda Michal editing with permission by Ernie Hawks)

Paradoxes of Life

Yesterday I called the dogs and said it was time for our hike to get the mail, a two mile, round-trip which is nearly always about the trek and not the mail. Each jumped up from their resting place and came running, jumping, wagging, and talking as they showed excitement to be included in an adventure.

There are several routes to the mailbox; the shortest and quickest is down the road, but shorter and quicker isn't always best so we headed north rather than west—the direction of our destination.

Callie is the smallest; she looks just like Benji (of movie fame) but is twice the size. Her method is to stay close and in sight but with forays away to follow a smell for a few seconds then right back—until the next smell attracts her. She may be the smallest but is the most aggressive if a bone, or some other tasty morsel, is found.

Glacier, the white German Shepherd, runs parallel to us almost out of sight. His coat is easy to see in the forest but is far enough away to only get a glimpse every minute or so. It's easy to track him because he is terrorizing squirrels who chatter, exposing his presence. However, with a call, or whistle, he is beside me.

Nikki, the biggest at about 90 pounds, stays close, stopping to sniff the weeds and grass at the edge of track we are on. Nikki looks like a Rhodesian Ridgeback mixed with everything else that must have been out that night. She is rarely out of sight and often under foot, but is as much a joy to be with as the others.

I enjoy each personality as they did their "wild thing" while still being obedient to my instructions. I never worry about them disappearing, or going on a chase; they all want to be with me but under their terms. I concur with those terms which makes the journey fun for us all.

The last hundred yards to the mailboxes is always on the road. Glacier explores a circle several feet wide around the boxes, Callie will check for new smells on the posts and trees close by, while Nikki will stop before we get there and wait. "Why go all the way and back? "she seems to say.

As I walk, the joy and companionship of these pets fills my thoughts with thankfulness for them and the life they have shared with me. Each one is part of the group while still being themselves. Nikki, in continual molt because she will not tolerate being brushed, wants to be close but still explore.

Callie, her long hair full of seed heads and her long ears flopping with each step, is checking out as much as possible without letting me out of her sight.

154

Glacier is a hot dog. He runs full tilt jumping logs, even off low cliffs. Running down steep hills he charges so fast he needs to take an occasional long leap for his feet to catch up with him.

Glacier and Callie lived together for only about two years, Nikki and Glacier only lived together about one year, Callie and Nikki were together for about four years. While they were together they complemented each other and had fun.

I usually take the short way home. As I approach our place each dog goes to its respective grave and lies down again. I wonder who else they had been running with while they were running with me.

The memory of my relationship with each and all of these four-legged friends is fresh in my mind. Glacier died in 2003, Callie in 2006. Just last Friday, Dr. Mike and Maggie came out and, while Nikki lay on her bed, she received her last shot. They even helped take her to the grave I had dug near her friends for her final rest. Their offer to lend a hand with the closing of the grave was turned down. Linda and I needed to do that alone.

On Saturday we were hiking one of our favorite trails. There is a log next to a small stream where we often sit and rest. Nikki liked the place as well; she would wade in and take a few laps of water then stand in the cool mud and rest her feet.

As we sat the air was filled with smells of the cycles of life. Dead vegetation was decomposing into nourishment for new life.

The day after we found out Nikki was terminal and in pain, two close friends got married in our back yard. It was a wonderful celebration about a new beginning while we anticipated our loss.

The day after the wedding we Skyped with Ana and Noah. It was fun to see the energy of our two-year-old granddaughter Alice Lindy. We also could see just how pregnant Ana was with Lucy Claire—another new life and new beginning. We are looking forward to being with them and to celebrating the arrival of Lucy in a few weeks.

All these events tell us of the complexities of our humanity. We can be excitedly happy while at the same time feel deep sadness. It is those pluralities of life that cannot be ignored and are not really individual. Rather, they are nearly always "both and."

Well, it's about time to get the mail again. One of these days Lucy and Alice will also do the trek with me. I wonder if they will see the ghost dogs that accompany us.

Alice still takes care of her baby doll and plays with her cars when she isn't helping with baby sister Lucy.

Being Prepared

It was the moment I had prepared for. I had done all the training, all the mental homework, all the Spiritual grounding. I had been getting ready for several weeks- now it was time. The door to our room opened, and the light of the hall back-lit Ana.

For the last week Navy jets have streaked low overhead in a tight formation, creating a screaming, rolling thunder across the partly cloudy sky. It is not a sound I am used when I am home, but it's very common in Virginia Beach, Virginia.

Back home in the woods of North Idaho a loud noise is a Pileated woodpecker's whack-whack-whack, or a coyote's brassy song announcing its presence.

But I was on a vacation (of sorts) in Virginia Beach, and thoroughly enjoying my time with Ana, Noah and Alice.

Noah and I enjoyed some beer we had brewed together last spring when I was there. He made sure some was saved for my return.

Alice and I had been playing in the parks and in the yard. I have been introduced to Dusty Plane of the Disney movie, as well as all of the cast of characters in the movie *Cars*; they are quite a fun bunch. We went for a bike ride around the neighborhood—well, she rode while I pushed the bike. It is a child's design with a handle on the back to push and steer. She got a good fun ride in. I got tired.

The real reason for being in Virginia Beach at this time is Ana, or more correctly, Lucy. Lucy was supposed arrive, via Ana, yesterday—so we were waiting.

For someone in tune to the timing and, what appears to be randomness of nature, this was a rather interesting experience for me. Our waiting seemed to be in sharp contrast to the jets that didn't even wait for their own sound waves.

I easily picked up on Ana's impatience and discomfort, while understanding there was nothing any of us could do to change the situation.

I may not have had any discomfort, except for tortured ears; still, I too felt anxious for the new baby's arrival, while at the same time loving the experience with family and a nearly three-year-old's energy, and sense of discovery of her world.

Back home, fall was painting a new landscape in our woods; the fawn's baby spots would be disappearing and maturing into the tawny brown of its parents. Occasionally, a small plane might fly high overhead, but the normal sounds are songs of nature getting ready for winter. Certainly from the perspective near a navy air base it is very calm and soothing.

As more jets roared overhead, Ana announced that she had given Lucy an eviction notice. It sounded good and I loved the imagery. We all knew Lucy was choosing her perfect birthday. So for another night we all headed to bed wondering if Lucy would chose that night or the morrow.

The hall light shined through the open door of our room as Ana walked in and said her contractions were close. It was time for action and each of us had agreed on a specific job; I knew all the others were ready, but was I? It was time for all my mental, Spiritual, and practical experience to be put to use.

Noah, Ana and Linda all moved quickly into their prearranged places - and drove off to the hospital.

A check of the clock said it was about 12:30 a.m. and I was left at home alone with Alice. She was sleeping so I tried to finish the night, but plans and routines were running through my head. I finally got up and took a shower so that would be behind me when she awoke. I loaded some toddler games onto my Kindle just in case all the preparation didn't work.

We had been with them for several days, and Alice and I had enjoyed some fun times together, but I wondered what her reaction would be to everyone being gone. Alice's mama had always been there when she got up, except for a couple times when Alice had stayed with us in Idaho.

She had been told Lucy Claire was growing in Mama's tummy and would come out soon and join the family. I still wasn't sure how she would act.

About 6 a.m. the baby monitor came to life with the sounds of a little girl getting out of bed. I went to the door of her room hoping for the best.

She looked at me and gave her cute cheery grin saying "Hi Gampa," then headed toward her mama and daddy's room.

I took a deep breath and said "Mama, Daddy and Grandma

have gone to the hospital because Lucy is coming out of Mama's tummy."

She said, "Otay," turned, and started down the stairs. I think that little girl was more prepared than I.

As we headed downstairs, her routine was running through my head. First I was to change her diaper, so I called her over and sat on the floor. That went well. A glass of juice was next. I got one for her, then found her playing with her cars and gave it to her.

Wondering how things were going to go I sat on the floor and played with her; she seemed to like that. She walked over to the television and reached for the button. I said, "You can't touch the button until after breakfast." She went back to her cars and juice.

"So far so good," I thought.

It seemed very quiet, and I realized the jets were not roaring overhead. I wondered if they were staying silent out of respect for Ana and Lucy. Probably not, but I had that thought.

A text came saying Ana was ready and pushing. A few minutes later another said Lucy was with us on this earth.

I said to Alice, "Sister Lucy is out of your mama's tummy."

She looked up at me and said, "otay." Then she came over to me and gave me a of her movie *Cars* character ,Mater, the tow truck or Tow Mater. I think she needed to reassure me everything was going to be okay or "otay."

After a breakfast of Cheerios with sliced strawberries, Linda came back. I had dressed Alice in her "Big Sister" t-shirt for the trip to see her new little sister.

Alice had a stuffed toy peacock as a gift for Lucy when she met her. So with that in hand, I put her in her car seat. As she was being strapped in she looked at the new baby seat next to her. It had never been there before. She said matter-of-factly, "That's Lucy's seat." How did she know?

At the hospital Alice commanded the doors to open with "Open Sesame." As I punched the auto door button, they opened,

Alice smiled and crossed the threshold. She charmed everyone in the hall as we walked hand in hand. As soon as we were in the room she climbed up on the bed with her mom and Lucy.

After a big hug Ana asked if Alice wanted to kiss her little sister; she did, and gave baby sis her first gift, the peacock.

Ana pointed to a bag of fun stuff and told Alice that Lucy had brought some gifts for her, too. Alice got down and taking a coloring book out of the present from Lucy, sat in the window seat and started working on it.

I finally turned my focus to Lucy, a perfect little bundle. The nurse who washed her said she was the mellowest baby the nurse has ever bathed at birth.

I gave Ana and Noah a hug and congratulated them; they exuded the love new parents show for their children and each other. Brushing away a tear I watched them be a family together.

Noah was at sea so didn't get to be at Alice's birth and was very excited to be on shore duty for Lucy. I understand from others in the room, there were a few tears from the sailor as baby Lucy arrived. Just as there was the first time he met his oldest daughter.

I was asked if I wanted to hold the newborn so I took her and sat down. I looked at her and she looked up at me. Once again, heart-opening love filled my soul. I knew Lucy Claire was in my heart forever just as her older sister was.

Alice came over and asked if she could hold baby Lucy. When Lucy was back on mom's lap, Alice climbed up again and sat on Ana's knee. Lucy was placed on Alice's lap with Mom holding both. Alice bent over and kissed her again, then straightened the birth cap on her little sis.

After a short visit Alice and I headed home again. When we arrived she went up to her room and found her baby doll, buried under some stuffed toys and had hardly been used. She brought the doll downstairs and said Baby Doll needed a diaper like Lucy. With that in place she said she needed a blanket like Lucy. Swaddled and diapered Baby Doll was put down to sleep and Alice started playing with her cars.

Alice still takes care of Baby Doll, and plays with her cars when she isn't helping with Baby Sister Lucy.

It appears she was much more prepared for the new experience than I and her only preparation was simply being Alice, while letting Lucy simply be Lucy. That is my lesson on dealing with anxiety.

After everyone was home and settled I went out and sat on the deck with a beer from Noah's batch. The jets were streaking across the sky again. I tried one of those toddler games on my Kindle. I may even master it soon.

High Holy Days

I often celebrate communion in the Cathedral of the Tamarack, Fir and Pine. The huge wooden columns reach up hundreds of feet to a high ceiling that is blue, or white or gray, or maybe a cloudy relief of all three. The floor is covered with thick, dark green moss, grasses and ferns that change color with the seasons and is blanketed with white in the winter. Often through the middle, a creek babbles toward some distant ocean as it cascades over rocks, bubbles under logs and splashes against the shore, creating music that accompanies a choir of finches, flickers and jays.

I believe God is everywhere, in all of us, and in everything, even beyond our understanding. This means a relationship with God includes people, animals and objects such as water, rocks, soil, plants and the air.

I believe in Divine Order, Creation if you will. There are arguments over whether it took seven days or several billion years to create this Earth. I lean toward several billion years, but then, I have friends who say I'm not fully evolved - maybe I'm hoping for some more time, or Divine Order.

We depend on the spirit in nature every minute of every day. Christina Baldwin writes in *The Seven Whispers,* "We start by calming ourselves, seeking peace of mind by taking in breath. And what is breath? Nature. Nature's gift: the exhalation of trees. As long as we are alive, the journey of spirituality always returns us to the body: we are of the earth."

I was scheduled to give a talk at a local church. The minister emailed the board saying he was going to be gone and to please support me in his absence. One member replied, "I'll be glad to support Ernie, unless the skiing looks good that day."

I strongly identify with that because I have often had spiritual experiences while others were in church, and generally they are unexpected. That is exactly what happened early one Sunday morning.

I was out and it was cold, in the low teens. My course took me along the frozen edge of a wetland. The steep bank on my right kept me from being there most of the year. On this day, the water the reed grass grew out of was frozen solid and made it possible to travel this route. What made this morning different was the cold snap had come before the snow's white blanket covered the land and obliterated the demarcation of the wetland's edge, and the slope where the forest climbed up the mountain.

As I walked along the frozen game trail, I saw a small silver-white spot just above the ice line on the bank, it was shiny and the size of a dollar coin. My curiosity was immediately piqued. I pushed through the frozen brittle stocks of grass, still standing in defiance of winter, until I reached the anomaly.

When I got on my knees, I could see a small burrow below a patch of frost, the result of the vapor of a small animal sleeping inside.

I didn't bother the little critter because I know how cranky I get when my sleep is interrupted.

I had never seen this phenomenon before. Then I thought,

"This may be the first time I've been out at this temperature without snow which would hide it."

As I hiked around the hills and through the valleys, I saw several more, some large patches of frost under the upper lip of large dens and many more of the dollar-sized spots.

This is nature. I didn't bother the animals; it would have been a violation. Curiosity is normal, but we need to be very careful and prayerful whenever we disrupt, or destroy, any part of nature. As Christina said, "We are of the earth."

Albert Schweitzer said, "Until he extends his circle of compassion to include all living things, man will not himself find peace." He said *all living things*: all of the earth, as well as all the plants and animals.

A winter trek is always a joy for me. If I were asked, I would have to say winter is on my list of top four favorite seasons.

Being out in the sweet, serene silence that only winter brings is refreshing and revitalizing. Searching for the mystery in the mists, enveloping streams flowing over frozen rocks and through icy, undomesticated landscapes, turns into a quiet session that lasts for hours.

These meetings with nature become church-like for me, not because many of them happen on Sunday morning, but because Spirit seems to scream through the silence at me. Then the petite song of a chickadee shatters the stillness with an announcement of its spirit.

During the dormant time of year, that includes some of the Holiest days for many people, it is easy for me to see the Christ in all of creation.

Once, sitting on a rock in the fog next to a fast-flowing stream, falling too quickly to freeze as its surroundings had, I studied the mist. A form seemed to be adding to the steam. I sat quietly as it moved through the haze. It was getting closer, moving and stopping. An image materialized. A shape I recognized began to develop, a bull elk. It took a step or two, browsed on an old leaf left on some brush, then moved closer to the stream. I could see the breath from his nostrils joining the mist over the stream. Then, I noticed my breath join the mist over the stream. The Christ in Elk, in Stream and in Me all created one cloud.

I wanted to shout out at that perfect image, "We *are* all one," but I didn't. It would have changed the whole scene. Elk needed to be there to browse and get a drink. Stream needed to be there to take the mountain energy down the valley. I needed to be there to get the message from Elk and Stream, and I wanted it to last as long as possible.

The book *Grandfather,* by Tom Brown Jr. says, "…you must understand that there can be no separation of nature and Spirit. They are one in the same. Nature becomes a doorway to the Spirit and Spirit also becomes a doorway to nature. There is only the sacred 'oneness' that we are all part of."

One excuse I use to experience the oneness is the quest for the perfect photo. I know it's the quest, not the photo that is important.

It is why I walked on snowshoes, before sunup, to a makeshift blind of mosquito netting I had put up the night before. It was on a slope level with the top of an old Bull Pine snag. I had seen bald eagles there several times.

I sat and waited, camera lens peeking through a slit in the netting. Enough light was coming over the mountains to see the lake at the base of the snag, a large, deep lake, which rarely froze. Ducks were on the water. An immature bald eagle appeared; the ducks rafted together in a tight little island as the youngster made an awkward and unsuccessful attempt to get breakfast.

I heard ravens winging over me, woodpeckers breaking the silence flying from tree to tree, but when I heard chickadees and nuthatches flitting in the brush around me, I knew I had been there long enough to be accepted.

The sun reached over the horizon and its rays made their way to the bottom of the valley and the water. Suddenly, the ducks scattered and flew as a mature Bald eagle sailed into my view, its wings set and gliding gracefully toward the water. Without a splash, a fish was grabbed and lifted toward the bare branch where my lens was trained. Eagle swooped up at the last minute, stalling as it grabbed the branch without letting go of its catch.

Several screeches gave thanks to Great Spirit and to the air that carried its wings, the rocks and soil for containing the lake, the trees for a safe place to roost and eat, the water for nurturing and growing this meal, and finally, a thanks to Fish for the gift of another day.

Then, reaching down with that big, yellow hooked beak, it took sustenance. I could hear the flesh tearing, bones breaking as Fish spirit gave Fish's Body to Eagle, and I felt honored to be allowed to witness the communion.

Thankfulness is imperative because we do leave a footprint. Fish gave its life so the eagle would survive. We also take life in our journey. It is easy to see if we eat meat as I do. I choose not to kill, but still, I am responsible for those lives where I take food, and it goes beyond that. When I eat a carrot, a spiritual being having an earthly experience ends. It will not grow or reproduce again.

In *Heart of Home,* from the essay "Carnivore, Omnivore, Vegan: The Hardest Questions", Ted Karasote writes, " If you want to stay in the game - meaning that you decide not to commit suicide and exempt yourself from all future killing - there isn't a single good strategy that lets you live without inflicting some harm. Neither carnivorism, omnivorism, nor vegetarianism are adequate solutions, nor is being an organic farmer, a careful livestock grower, or an aboriginal hunter-gatherer. Some life plans, of course, are more clear-sighted than others. Whichever we choose, we can try to take gently those lives that support us, offering thanks for their gifts, and rejoicing often that we are given another day."

Now, please, don't feel guilty for living. My hope for you

is to raise your awareness even more.

My hope for you is to appreciate and honor Spirit in all its forms, while walking consciously through this plane.

My hope for you is to understand how we are dependent on nature while we take from it and take care of it.

Let me give you an example of caring for nature while using her resources.

Linda and I are blessed by our forest and we understand that it needs our care and blessing. It was neglected for several years after having been brutally logged. We are strengthening the whole woods through careful selective logging, selling some, using others to rebuild and warm our home. We start by thanking each tree we take, promising to not knowingly waste anything.

An important piece of maintenance is slash and spread. The parts of the trees that we can't use are cut up and spread on the forest floor, becoming natural fertilizer as they decompose back into the earth. They nurture and support the brothers, and sisters, and children, and grandchildren, of the trees we take.

How does Spirit in nature bless you? If you have never had the opportunity to feel the energy of a mature tree, or a rock, or the earth, I hope you get it soon. Putting yourself in direct contact with them is a way to experience the blessings of nature, and feel the energy. And the intention of your energy blesses nature.

The pictures of Eagle and Fish were lame, but the images were seared into my soul. I sat there for most of the rest of the day, thinking about the dens and the frost, about Elk and his lesson of oneness and I gave thanks to Great Spirit for the High Holy Days. Leaning against one of those giant columns in the Cathedral of the Tamarack, Fir and Pine, feeling its energy, I rejoiced in having been given another day.

This story first appeared in Science of Mind magazine

Made in the USA
San Bernardino, CA
19 May 2014